WESTERN LITURGIES

WESTERN LITURGIES

BY

R. C. WEST, A.K.C.

LONDON
SOCIETY FOR PROMOTING
CHRISTIAN KNOWLEDGE
NEW YORK: THE MACMILLAN COMPANY

PREFACE

THE object of this little book is to put before the interested reader an English translation of the Western Liturgies. Much has been written about the Liturgies contained in this book, thus the portion given to introducing the various rites is necessarily brief, as fuller information can be easily obtained in the text-books.

I am very grateful to the Oxford University Press for permission to use C. E. Hammond's *Antient Liturgies* as the basis for the translations of the Roman, Ambrosian, Gallican, and Mozarabic rites, and for permission to use the text of the Celtic rites given in F. E. Warren's *Liturgy and Ritual of the Celtic Church*. I am also very grateful to Dr. Leighton Pullan for permission to use his version of the Mozarabic Canon which is given in his *History of the Book of Common Prayer*. I am greatly indebted to the valuable help rendered by the Rev. G. B. White of Birmingham, in checking my work with regard to the Celtic rites. Finally, I owe a great deal to Dr. Lowther Clarke, who has taken a great interest in the production of this book, and made many very helpful and valuable suggestions; and also I would like to express my sincere thanks to the press reader of the Oxford University Press, who has taken an interest in this work and given advice which I greatly appreciate.

R. C. WEST.

BANBURY, OXON.
  October 1938.

CONTENTS

INTRODUCTION

I. THE ROMAN LITURGY

THE origin of the Roman Liturgy is somewhat obscure, but writers are more or less agreed that the present rite is a re-organized edition of a primitive Liturgy in fairly general use throughout the undivided Christian Church. Fortescue thinks that out of this primitive but fluid rite all the old Liturgies are derived.[1] From the time of Justin Martyr (c. 150) and the *Apostolic Tradition* of Hippolytus (225) there is no evidence at all either in support of or in opposition to this theory. It would seem from the famous treatise *De Sacramentis* that the chief changes came about some time during the fourth century. This treatise is a valuable witness for the Canon of the Mass, and contains some sections of the Canon now in use.

The language of the Roman Church for the first two and a half centuries was Greek. It is therefore highly probable that its Liturgy was also Greek. At what time the transition from Greek to Latin took place is not easy to estimate. No doubt the two languages were spoken side by side for a period, and the process was gradual. In 360 a certain writer, Marius Victorinus Africanus, quotes a liturgical prayer in Greek.[2] Some writers seem to think that the Liturgy was recast at the time of the language change.

The three most important books for the history of the Roman rite are the *Leonine Sacramentary*, the *Gelasian*, and the *Gregorian*. The first is a collection of Propers, i.e. Collects, Secrets, Post-communions, &c., but does not contain an *Ordo* or Canon. The manuscript is incomplete: there are no Masses before April, and we have none of the Easter ceremonies. It is a purely Roman book, and does not therefore contain any of the later Gallican additions. It has been attributed to Pope Leo (440–61), but there is no evidence to show that it is his work; in fact it has been said that he added certain words to the Canon, thus implying that the Canon was already in existence.

[1] Fortescue, *The Mass*, p. 53.   [2] Probst, *Abendländische Messe*, p. 5.

The Gelasian Sacramentary, named after Pope Gelasius (492–6), is a Roman book which has been Gallicanized; there is no special reason for mentioning the name of Gelasius, as none of the manuscripts bear this title, but tradition has it that Gelasius wrote a sacramentary, and it is possible that the kernel of this work may be his. There are various theories as to its origin which are dealt with in Fortescue's book.[1]

The Gregorian Sacramentary. Charles the Great in 791 sent to Pope Adrian I for a copy of the Roman Church's Sacramentary, and Adrian sent one, which Charles introduced throughout his kingdom. This copy was the Gregorian Sacramentary. However, many of the Gallican customs were too popular to suppress, so these were added for use in the Frankish kingdom.[2] In the course of time this supplement came to be combined with the original work received from Rome, and eventually returned to Rome in this mixed form,[3] where it was adopted and has been kept with minor additions to the present day. Thus, so far as the *Ordo* and Canon are concerned, there have been no essential changes in the Roman Liturgy since the introduction of this book. Gregory's part in the original work was to revise, condense, and reorganize the Gelasian Sacramentary. He is also responsible for the addition of the phrase 'dispose our days in thy peace, that we may be delivered from eternal damnation and be numbered in the flock of thine elect' to the Canon. He also placed the Lord's Prayer at the close of the Canon, where it had been displaced by the Fraction. He argued that the most solemn act of consecration was performed by man-made formula, and that the prayer which our Lord had Himself taught us did not accompany this act. The Ambrosian Canon displays the old order in this respect.

Gradually the Roman rite spread throughout the West, displacing the Gallican rites. The process began before the time of Charles the Great and went on until the final extinction by a decree of King Pepin in the eighth century; his action is mentioned in a document of Charles the Great in 789. The Roman rite was introduced into England, and later into Scotland and Ireland;

---

[1] *The Mass*, p. 121.   [2] Ibid., p. 122.
[3] Pullan, *History of the Book of Common Prayer*, p. 19.

hence we get the rise of local rites such as 'Sarum', 'Hereford', 'York', &c. After the Reformation the Roman Missal was reformed by Pius V, who restored the old Roman rite, purging it of the later medieval developments, and this revised Missal is the one now in use in the Roman Church. There have been later revisions, but they are of little importance so far as the texts of the *Ordo* and Canon are concerned.

Bibliography

A. FORTESCUE. *The Mass.* Longmans, 1937.
C. E. HAMMOND. *Antient Liturgies.* Oxford, 1878.
L. DUCHESNE. *Christian Worship.* S.P.C.K., 1919.
E. BISHOP. *Liturgica Historica.* Oxford, 1918.
G. DIX. *The Apostolic Tradition of Hippolytus.* S.P.C.K., 1937.
L. PULLAN. *History of the Book of Common Prayer.* Longmans, 1929.

2. THE AMBROSIAN LITURGY

The early history of the Ambrosian rite is somewhat uncertain. Tradition ascribes it to S. Ambrose, Bishop of Milan (374–97), but, as Fortescue points out, a liturgy is not really composed by one man but is a development of gradual evolution.[1] The rite as we have it is much Romanized, but it is possible to eliminate the Roman portions and gain a clear conception of the original Milanese rite.

Writers are at variance as to which of the 'families' this rite belongs to. Pullan thinks that it is a Gallican Liturgy:[2] Hammond, on the other hand, inclined to the view that it was an independent and parallel development of the early Latin Roman Liturgy, which has been considerably influenced by the Roman See. Duchesne considers it to be the starting-point of all the Gallican family, and holds that it was derived from Antioch. Neale thinks that it is a branch of the Ephesine family, but moulded by contact with the Petrine Liturgy.[3] The present writer is inclined to the view that it is a Gallican rite, as it contains the Gallican features even with regard to the Canon used on Maundy Thursday and Easter eve. These are definitely Gallican and exhibit the older

[1] *The Mass*, p. 106, note 3. [2] *H.B.C.P.*, p. 20.
[3] *Essays on Liturgiology*, p. 171.

local Anaphora. The Canon in general use represents an older type than the Gregorian, and the Lord's Prayer is to be found here in the place where Gregory knew it before he altered its position.

There are traces of Greek influence in the 'Prayer over the Corporal'; the Deacon's proclamation of silence previous to the reading of the Epistle; the Litanies which are in use on the Sundays in Lent; the paragraph after the consecration of the wine, 'As oft as ye shall do this', &c.; and the saying of the Creed after the Offertory, which is an Eastern characteristic.

The rite was used originally throughout the whole diocese of Milan. Charles the Great desired to introduce the Roman Liturgy there as well, but the opposition was too great and the importance of the See together with the great name of S. Ambrose attached to the Liturgy, and the loyalty of the people to their rite, made this impracticable. Several subsequent attempts to introduce the Roman rite at Milan have also failed.[1] The Ambrosian Liturgy is now used in the whole of the old archdiocese of Milan, and in a few parts of the Swiss Canton of Ticino.

Bibliography

NEALE. *Essays on Liturgiology*. 1867. pp. 171 ff.
BISHOP. *The Mozarabic and Ambrosian Rites*. 1924.
DUCHESNE. *Christian Worship*. S.P.C.K., 1919.

3. THE GALLICAN RITE

When we come to consider this rite we are at once confronted with a difficulty, because, although there are several manuscripts of this use, we do not possess one that gives us an *Ordo*. The documents that we possess are largely Sacramentaries, i.e. the variable parts of the Liturgy. The chief sources of information on the rite, from which the Liturgy translated below is derived, are contained in the *Missale Gothicum*, the *Missale Gallicanum Vetus*, the *Letters of S. Germain of Paris*, and the *Bobbio Missal*. We will therefore deal with these first.

1. *The Missale Gothicum* was drawn up for use in the Church of Autun. It is not a pure Gallican book at all, for it contains

---

[1] *The Mass*, p. 180.

many Roman elements. The various formularies are given in the order which the Gallican Mass followed. It is not complete, as two Masses are missing at the beginning, and it ends after the first prayer in a *Missa Cotidiana Romensis*. No precise date can be fixed to the Missal, but, as it contains a Mass in honour of S. Leger, who was Bishop of Autun and died in 680, it cannot be older than the closing years of the seventh century or the early years of the eighth.

2. *The Missale Gallicanum Vetus* is likewise not a pure Gallican book, as it too contains many Roman additions. It is much mutilated, but is of value in the sense that it contains the ceremonies of Holy Week and Easter. It is the same date as the *Missale Gothicum* and contains a Mass in honour of S. Germain of Auxerre.

3. *The Letters of S. Germain.* These letters are of the greatest importance for our purposes as they are the only remaining account of the Liturgy, and it is from this source that we are enabled to reconstruct the order of the service. The letters have been attributed to S. Germain, who was Bishop of Paris from 555 to 576. The first of these letters has as its title: 'Germane bishop of Paris has written about the Mass'. In our time the authorship has been disputed. Mgr. Duchesne as late as 1919 still saw good reasons to attribute them to Germain, but Fr. Thurston in a foreword to Fortescue's book *The Mass* points out that we can no longer connect these letters with S. Germain, but draws attention to Dom Wilmart's theory which says that they were not written until a hundred years later.[1] However, they are still the only real guide which enables us to reconstruct the Liturgy.

The Bobbio Missal. This Missal is so called because it was discovered by Mabillon at Bobbio and was published by him in vol. i of his *Museum Italicum*. It is also published in the Henry Bradshaw Society's texts. It begins with a 'Mass to be said Daily' which contains the Lections, Prayers, &c., to be used on days for which no other Mass is prescribed. All the formularies up to the Preface are Gallican, the Canon is Gregorian, and the

[1] Ibid., p. xii. For a complete discussion see Dom Wilmart in the *Dictionnaire d'Archéologie et de Liturgie*, vol. vi, cc. 1049–102. Duchesne's version is in *Christian Worship*, pp. 155, 189–227.

conclusion is Roman. A noticeable feature of the book is that all the Masses end at the Sanctus; thus it would seem that they all concluded in the same way as the Mass for daily use. The date is sixth or seventh century.

In addition to these documents on the Gallican rite there are a few fragments of sacramentaries which have been published by Mone. There are eleven Masses in all, which were found in the library at Karlsruhe in a palimpsest manuscript, which once belonged to the Abbey of Reichenau, and is commonly known as the *Missale Reichenovense*.[1] There is also a lectionary known as the *Luxoviensis*, so called because it was discovered by Mabillon at the Abbey of Luxeuil, and published by him in his *De Liturgia Gallicana*. This is a pure Gallican book without any traces of Roman influence.[2]

The Gallican rite was suppressed at the beginning of the ninth century, and until Cardinal Thomasius, in the seventeenth century, published three sacramentaries containing Gallican elements, it was not known that any relics of this use were in existence.

The Gallican Liturgy is interesting to students of English Liturgies and Church history, from the point of view that it was during the course of a similar service as printed below that the first Archbishop of Canterbury, S. Augustine, was consecrated.

It will be hardly necessary to describe the rite in detail as this has already been done by other writers;[3] it will be sufficient to point out a few characteristic elements in the service. (1) The Salutation 'The Lord be with you' has the addition of the word *semper*, i.e. 'always' or 'ever'. This is a typical Gallican method of giving the Salutation, and it is also found in the Mozarabic rite. (2) The Liturgy contained a Litany as in the Eastern rites; but this is not given in the Missals. The Stowe Missal, however, gives one, and it should be compared with the Litanies in the Clementine Liturgy, where it will be noticed that they are closely related. It is quite probable that the Gallican Litanies or *Preces* are in the main translations almost verbatim of the

[1] Hammond, *Antient Liturgies*, p. lxviii.
[2] Duchesne, *Christian Worship*, p. 154.
[3] Ibid.

Deacon's Litany in the Eastern rites.[1] (3) The Oblations were prepared beforehand and brought in at the Offertory in procession by the Deacon or one of the Sacred Ministers in a silver vessel shaped like a tower (4) The Diptychs were read before the Canon proper began. (5) The words of the Canon were not given in full, only the opening words of the recital of the institution. This is no doubt accounted for by the fact that, since the Celebrant would know the words by heart, the scribes did not consider it necessary to write the complete form. (6) The Preface to the Lord's Prayer is a variable form In the Roman rite there is a fixed form, but in the Gallican rite the form would vary with the Mass. It is interesting to note that in the Bobbio Missal the original form was 'Instructed by the Divine teaching, and [following] Divine instruction we are bold to say'. This has been altered in the manuscript by the scribe in conformity with the Roman use to read 'Admonished by salutary precepts', &c. Mabillon is certain that the prayer was said, not by the Priest alone, but also by the people present. (7) The *Embolismos* of the Lord's Prayer varies with the Mass. In the Roman rite it is a fixed form.

The majority of the passages in the following text which appear in brackets are not in the original texts, but are merely inserted here in order to explain the various portions of the service. We do not know what the original rubrics were, so that at best they are mere reconstructions from the various sources at our disposal.

No examples of Antiphons, Graduals, Communions, &c., can be given, for the reason that no Gallican 'Antiphonary' has ever been discovered.

4. THE MOZARABIC RITE

The word 'Mozarabic' has been much discussed, and it would seem to be derived from an Arabic word *musta'rab*, which means 'those who assume the manners of Arabs'.[2] The name 'Mozarabic' was given to those Christians in Spain who lived under

[1] Trans. of Clementine Liturgy by Cresswell (S.P.C.K.).
[2] Pullan, *H.B.C.P.*, p. 327.

Arab rule. It is to be found now in use only in a chapel of the Cathedral at Toledo, where it is kept alive by a college of chaplains.

The rite is essentially the old Spanish rite slightly Romanized. The Spanish liturgy was revised and re-edited by Cardinal Ximenes in 1500 at a time when the Roman rite was driving it into the background. The original rite has been attributed to Isidore of Seville (560–636), and in a work by him, *De Ecclesiasticis Officiis*, the Mass is fully described and explained. In point of fact, it is highly improbable that Isidore did actually compose this Liturgy, but more probably he arranged and perfected it. Hammond says: 'to whatever period we are to assign the first organization of a Christian Church in Spain, to the same period belonged a first form of that Liturgy which, by the labours of Isidore, Leander, and others was developed into the "Mozarabic" Liturgy'.[1]

The text translated below is from Migne's *Patrologia Latina*, tt. lxxxi, lxxxii, as given in Hammond's book, *Antient Liturgies*. This text gives a clear idea of some of the Roman insertions. The following are the main instances of such additions. (1) The Confession and Introit at the beginning of the Office: as in the old rite this comes before the Illation. (2) There is a double elevation. According to the old rite the first was placed shortly after the Consecration, and immediately prior to the Creed. The other was inserted in the Roman rite at the close of the words of Consecration. (3) The usual Commemoration of the Living and the Dead occurs as in the Gallican rite immediately after the Offertory; a second Commemoration for the Living appears after the Consecration.

Another noticeable point about this Liturgy is the double ending of the prayers, i.e. at the conclusion of the petitions the Choir respond 'Amen', then the Celebrant says a Doxology, and again the Choir respond with a second 'Amen'. The ceremony of the 'Fraction' is rather unusual and is not to be found in this form in other Liturgies.

Bibliography

DUCHESNE. *Christian Worship*. S.P.C.K., 1919.
LESLIE. *Patrologia Latina*. (Ed.) in Migne.
NEALE. *Essays in Liturgiology*.

[1] Hammond, *Antient Liturgies*, p. lxiv.

5. THE CELTIC LITURGIES

The phrase 'Celtic Church' means that branch of the Catholic Church in Great Britain and Ireland before the coming of S. Augustine. In central England the Celtic Church became extinct at the end of the fifth century, owing to wars or invasions having driven the members to the remoter parts of the country. It survived, however, in the Devon and Somerset area, and in Wales, Scotland, and Ireland, for at least two more centuries, until it gradually submitted to the Roman rule. It remained independent for some time in Ireland, and it was not until 1172, at the Synod of Cashel, that the Sarum form of the Roman use was ordered to be introduced into every church in Ireland.[1]

The exact date when Christianity first came to the British Isles is uncertain, but it can be placed between 176 and 208. Irenaeus compiled a list of Churches in 176, but made no allusion to the Celtic Church. In 208 Tertullian alluded to the existence of Christianity in these isles. 'Galliarum diversae nationes, et Britannorum inaccessa Romanis loca Christo vero subdita . . .' (*Adv. Jud.* vii). The persecution in Lyons and Vienne in 177 may have brought Christians from Gaul to Britain. It is also quite conceivable that there were numbers of Roman soldiers in the army of occupation who would have left some converts from among those with whom they associated.[2]

The most complete relic of the Celtic Church and its Liturgy is to be found in the *Stowe Missal*. This is an Irish manuscript written in two hands, one probably eighth and the other tenth century. It takes its name from the fact that it was discovered abroad in the eighteenth century, and remained until 1849 at the Stowe Library in the possession of the Duke of Buckingham. It is now in the library of the Earl of Ashburnham, at Ashburnham Place.[3]

There is a detailed account of this Missal in Warren's *Liturgy and Ritual of the Celtic Church*, but the main points to note here

[1] Warren, *Liturgy and Ritual of the Celtic Church*, pp. 1–11.
[2] On the question of Christianity's coming to these isles see Wakeman, *History of the Church of England*, pp. 1 ff.
[3] Warren, op. cit., p. 199.

are: (*a*) The rubrics are few in number, and they are written in Irish and not Latin, as is the actual text. (*b*) The presence of a Litany between the Epistle and Gospel, which is a sign of Gallican influence. (*c*) The absence of the 'Filioque' from the Creed. (*d*) An unchanging Epistle and Gospel. (*e*) The Canon is headed 'Canon dominicus papae Gilasi', but is in reality the 'Gregorian Canon' with the addition of a long list of Irish saints. In the translation following, all the names are not given, only a short selection. (*f*) The Fraction precedes the Lord's Prayer as it did before the alteration effected by Gregory. In addition to these points of interest, it is interesting to note a rubric which mentions only a partial uncovering of the Chalice; also the rubric which says 'Here is amplification'. This in the text reads 'Hic augmentum', and 'augmentum' is a rare word used by Arnobius, *Adv. Gentes*, lib. vii, c. 24.[1] It may mean that the unwritten conclusion to the Collect follows here, or it may be that it signifies that the Priest may say some additional prayer at this point of the service.

The Book of Deer

This fragment is a portion of the Service for the Communion of the Sick, which appears to have been written some time previous to 1130 on a vacant space in the *Book of Deer*. This is a book of the Gospels. The short Eucharistic Office which it contains shows a marked resemblance to the Mozarabic and Gallican Missals. This is a Scottish fragment, and Warren is of the opinion that it affords evidence that the Scoto-Pictish Liturgy of the Columban Church in Scotland belonged to the 'Ephesine' family rather than the 'Petrine'.[2]

The Book of Dimma

This is an Irish fragment, attributed to one Dimma, who lived in the seventh century. It has been attributed to that date for that reason. It is written between the Gospels of S. Luke and S. John on ff. 52–4 of the *Book of Dimma* now in the library of Trinity College, Dublin. As will be seen, it is a *Missa de Infirmis*.

[1] See Warren, op. cit., p. 251, note 16.   [2] Ibid., p. 163.

The Book of Mulling

There is yet another fragment written in the *Book of Mulling*, which is ascribed to Mulling, who was Bishop of Ferns and died in 697. It contains the ascription 'nomen scriptoris Mulling'. The manuscript is now in the library of Trinity College, Dublin. The fragment is written in a ninth-century hand at the end of S. Matthew's Gospel. It is a form of Communion and Unction of the Sick (*Missa de Infirmis*).

Bibliography

WARREN. *Liturgy and Ritual of the Celtic Church.* Oxford, 1881. Gives a further list of references.

6. THE SARUM RITE

After the coming of S. Augustine to England in 597, the Gallican Liturgy was gradually superseded by the Roman rite. This in turn yielded, though not without a struggle, to the influence of the French Liturgies which came over with the Normans. Thus it came to pass that there was no uniformity in this country with regard to the Liturgy, each diocese having its own use. The most important of these diocesan uses were Hereford, York, and Sarum. The latter is far the most important, as in time it came to be introduced not only in the greater part of England but also in Scotland and Ireland.

The Sarum rite used to be attributed to S. Osmund, who became Bishop of Salisbury in 1078, but it is more likely that the liturgical work was carried out by Richard Poore (1210), who was first Dean and then Bishop of Salisbury.

At the beginning of the tenth century five dioceses were formed out of the original Wessex, of which Ramsbury and Sherborne were two. These two became amalgamated in 1058, under Herman, and were transferred to Sarum. In his time the Cathedral body was secular and not monastic, but when Osmund became Bishop it became monastic, and the Norman idea of a Chapter was set up. This was new to English minds, as previously the Bishop sat in the apsidal end of his church with the clergy, to transact the business of the church. Now the necessity for the prolonged absence of the Bishop from his church was greater, and so the Chapter had to be made a separate body, under the Dean. S. Osmund instituted under Royal Sanction a Cathedral Chapter, and copies of the documents of institution remain.[1] These are known as the 'Charter of Osmund' and the 'Institution'.

In Poore's time the 'Consuetudinary' was drawn up, which is a book of rules for the dignity and duties of the residentiary clergy. It is possible that this document contains some of S. Osmund's liturgical prescriptions. Another instrument, known as the 'Customary', was drawn up, which was based on the 'Consuetudinary'. Later this was combined with another document, the 'Ordinal', which was a book for use by the choir, and also served as a guide for the other service books. From the combination of the two the rubrics of the Sarum books were taken.

The Sarum Missal remains in various editions: and the one used in the translation is the 1526 edition. The rubrics have been considerably condensed, as they are often very long and full of minute details. I have contented myself with giving merely the *Ordo*, as the Canon is the same in an English version as that of the Roman. There are only a few very slight verbal differences. It is in the variable portions of the Liturgy that the variations are great and of importance. It will be noticed that the Kiss of Peace is given in the preparation of the Priest and his Ministers at the beginning of the Mass. At the end of the Canon different prayers are prescribed for the Priest's Communion from those in the Roman rite. The 'Last Gospel' is to be said on the way back to the vestry, whereas in the Roman it is said before leaving the altar.

[1] See Frere, *Use of Sarum*, vol. i, p. 257, for a full account of the origin of the Sarum use.

I. THE ROMAN LITURGY

As soon as the Priest is ready he proceeds to the altar; having made a reverence, he signs himself with the sign of the cross from the forehead to the breast and says aloud:

In the Name of the Father, and of the Son, and of the Holy Ghost. Amen.

Then with hands joined before his breast, he begins the Antiphon.
I will go unto the altar of God.

The Ministers:
Unto the God of my joy and gladness.

Afterwards he says alternately with the Ministers the following Psalm.
Give sentence with me, O God, &c. Psalm 43.[1]
Glory be to the Father, &c.
As it was in the beginning, &c.

The Priest repeats the Antiphon. I will go unto the altar of God.
R̂. Even unto the God of my joy and gladness.

He signs himself, saying: Our help standeth in the name of the Lord.
R̂. Who hath made heaven and earth.[2]

Then bowing down humbly, he makes the Confession, with joined hands.

(*In Masses of the Dead and in Masses from Passion Sunday to Holy Saturday exclusive the Psalm* Give sentence with me *with* Glory be to the Father *and the repetition of the Antiphon is omitted; but having said* In the Name of the Father, I will go, *and* Our help, *he makes the following Confession:*)

I confess to God Almighty, to blessed Mary ever Virgin, to blessed Michael the Archangel, to blessed John the Baptist, to the holy Apostles Peter and Paul, to all the Saints and to you,

---

[1] The Psalm numbers and the version throughout this book are taken from the English Book of Common Prayer.   [2] Ps. 124[7].

brethren, that I have sinned exceedingly, in thought, word, and deed. *He strikes his breast three times, saying:* through my fault, through my fault, through my most grievous fault. Wherefore I pray blessed Mary ever Virgin, blessed Michael the Archangel, blessed John the Baptist, the holy Apostles Peter and Paul, all the Saints, and you, brethren, to pray for me to the Lord our God.

The Ministers respond:

May Almighty God have mercy upon thee, forgive thee thy sins, and bring thee to everlasting life.

The Priest says Amen *and raises himself.*

Then the Ministers repeat the Confession, and where it was said by the Priest and to you, brethren, *and* you, brethren, *is said to* you, Father, *and* you, Father.

Afterwards the Priest with joined hands gives the Absolution, saying:

May Almighty God have mercy upon you, forgive you your sins, and bring you to everlasting life.

℟. Amen.

He signs himself with the sign of the cross, saying:

May the Almighty and merciful Lord grant us pardon, absolution, and remission of our sins.

℟. Amen.

And bowing down he proceeds:

℣. Wilt thou not turn and quicken us, O Lord;

℟. That thy people may rejoice in thee?[1]

℣. Shew us thy mercy, O Lord;

℟. And grant us thy salvation.[2]

℣. O Lord, hear my prayer;

℟. And let my cry come unto thee.

℣. The Lord be with you;

℟. And with thy spirit.

And extending and joining his hands he says in a clear voice Let us pray, *and going up to the altar he says secretly:*

Take away from us we beseech thee, O Lord, our iniquities,

[1] Ps. 85⁶. [2] Ps. 85⁷.

that we may be worthy to enter the Holy of Holies with pure minds. Through Christ our Lord. Amen.

Then with joined hands and bowing over the altar he says:

We pray thee, O Lord, through the merits of thy Saints, *he kisses the altar in the middle*, whose relics are here, and of all the Saints; that thou wouldest vouchsafe to forgive me all my sins. Amen.

(In Solemn Masses the Celebrant, before he reads the Introit, blesses the Incense, saying: By him be thou blessed, in whose honour thou shalt be burned. Amen. *And when he has taken the thurible from the Deacon, he censes the altar, saying nothing. Afterwards the Deacon, when he has taken the thurible from the Celebrant, censes him only.)*

Then the Celebrant signing himself with the sign of the cross begins the Introit.

[*e.g. The First Mass of Christmas.*

The Lord hath said unto me: Thou art my Son, this day have I begotten thee.[1]

Ps. Why do the heathen so furiously rage together: and why do the people imagine a vain thing?[2]

Which being finished is repeated: The Lord hath said, *as far as the Psalm.*

This method of repeating the Introit is observed throughout the whole year. Glory be to the Father, *however, is omitted in Masses from Passion Sunday until Easter*.]

When the Introit is finished he says alternately with the Ministers:

Kyrie eleison. Kyrie eleison. Kyrie eleison.

Christe eleison. Christe eleison. Christe eleison.

Kyrie eleison. Kyrie eleison. Kyrie eleison.

Afterwards in the midst of the altar, extending and joining his hands, and bowing his head a little, he says, if it is to be said, and continues with hands joined:

Glory be to God on high. And in earth peace, to men of good will. We praise thee, we bless thee, we adore thee (*he bows his*

[1] Ps. 2[7].   [2] Ps. 2[1].

head). We glorify thee, we give thanks to thee (*he bows his head*) for thy great glory, O Lord God, heavenly King, God the Father Almighty. O Lord, the only-begotten Son, Jesu Christ (*he bows his head*), O Lord God, Lamb of God, Son of the Father, that takest away the sins of the world, have mercy upon us. Thou that takest away the sins of the world, have mercy upon us. Thou that takest away the sins of the world, receive our prayer (*he bows his head*). Thou that sittest at the right hand of God the Father, have mercy upon us. For thou only art holy; thou only art the Lord; thou only, O Christ, with the Holy Ghost, art most high in (*he bows his head*) the glory of God the Father. Amen.

Thus is the Gloria in excelsis *said also in Masses of the Blessed Mary, when it is to be said. It is recited in Masses between the season of Advent, from Septuagesima until Easter, except Feria V in the Feast of the Lord and Holy Saturday, in all Vigils, in Masses of the Dead, in all Votive Masses, in Ferial Offices, &c.*

The Angelic Hymn being finished he kisses the altar in the middle, and turns to the people and says:

The Lord be with you;

℞. And with thy spirit.

Afterwards he says Let us pray *and one or more* Prayers *as the Office requires.*

The Epistle *follows, which being finished* Thanks be to God *is responded by the Ministers. If it has been taken from the Acts of the Apostles, he begins:* In those days, *if from the Epistles:* Brethren, *if from the Pastoral Epistles of Paul,* Beloved, &c. *Sometimes, as in the four Ember seasons, more lections are read before the Epistle, chiefly from the Old Testament, separated by prayers.*

After the Epistle the Gradual *is said, after the Gradual two* Alleluias *are said, then a* Verse, *and after the Verse one* Alleluia.

[*e.g. The Nativity First Mass.*

In the day of thy power shall the people offer thee free will offerings with an holy worship: the dew of thy birth is of the womb of the morning.[1]

[1] Ps. 110[3].

℣. The Lord said unto my Lord: sit thou on my right hand, until I make thine enemies thy footstool.[1]

Alleluia. Alleluia. The Lord hath said unto me: Thou art my Son, this day have I begotten thee.[2] Alleluia.]

[*In Eastertide the Gradual is often not said, but two verses are said, e.g. Second Sunday after Easter:*

Alleluia. Alleluia.

℣. The disciples knew the Lord Jesus in the breaking of bread. Alleluia.[3]

℣. I am the good shepherd, and know my sheep, and am known of mine.[4] Alleluia.

From Septuagesima until Holy Saturday Alleluia *is not said; neither is it said in Masses of Ferials in Advent, &c. During Lent in place of it is said the* Tract *after this manner:*

He hath not dealt with us after our sins: nor rewarded us according to our wickednesses.[5]

℣. O remember not our old sins, but have mercy upon us and that soon: for we are come to great misery.

℣. Help us, O God of our salvation, for the glory of thy Name: O deliver us, and be merciful unto our sins, for thy Name's sake.[6]

The aforesaid Tract is said from Ash Wednesday until Feria IV in Holy Week, unless a Proper is assigned.]

In the Resurrection of the Lord after the Gradual is said the Sequence, *the* Paschal Victim; *at* Pentecost, Come, Holy Ghost; *on the Festival of Corpus Christi,* Sion, lift up thy voice and sing; *in Masses for the Dead,* O day of wrath.

These things being finished, if it is a Solemn Mass, the Deacon places the Gospel Book down on the middle of the altar, and the Celebrant blesses the incense as above; then the Deacon kneels before the altar with hands joined and says:

Cleanse my heart and my lips, O Almighty God, who didst cleanse the lips of the prophet Isaiah with a burning coal; and

---

[1] Ps. 110[1].   [2] Ps. 2[7].   [3] Based on Luke 24[31].
[4] John 10[14].   [5] Ps. 103[10].   [6] Ps. 79[8-9].

C

vouchsafe through thy gracious mercy so to purify me, that I may worthily proclaim thy holy Gospel. Through Christ our Lord.

Afterwards he takes the Book from the altar, and again kneels and asks a blessing from the Priest, saying:

Pray, sir, a blessing.

The Priest replies:

The Lord be in thy heart and on thy lips, that thou mayest worthily and rightly proclaim his holy Gospel. In the name of the Father, and of the Son ✠, and of the Holy Ghost. Amen.

And having received the blessing he kisses the Celebrant's hand, and with the other Ministers, the incense and the lights, approaching the Gospel place, standing with joined hands, he says:

The Lord be with you;

℞. And with thy spirit.

And proclaiming: The continuation of the Holy Gospel according to N. or the beginning of . . . *With the thumb of his right hand he signs the Book at the beginning of the Gospel, which he is about to read, then he signs himself on his forehead, mouth, and breast, and whilst the Ministers reply,* Glory be to thee, O Lord, *he censes the Book three times; afterwards he continues the Gospel with joined hands; when it is finished the Subdeacon carries the Book to the Priest, who kisses the Gospel saying:* By the words of the Gospel may our sins be blotted out. *Then the Priest is censed by the Deacon.*

If in fact the Priest celebrates without a Deacon and Subdeacon, when the Book has been carried to the other side of the altar, having bowed in the midst, he says with hands joined: Cleanse my heart (*as above*) *and* Pray, sir, a blessing. The Lord be in my heart and on my lips, that I may worthily and rightly proclaim his Gospel. Amen. *Then having turned towards the Book he says with joined hands:* The Lord be with you. ℞. And with thy spirit, *and proclaiming* The beginning *or* The continuation of the Holy Gospel, &c., *he signs the Book and himself on the forehead, mouth, and breast, and reads the Gospel, as has been said. When it is finished the Minister responds:* Praise be to thee, O Christ; *and the Priest kisses the Gospel, saying:* By the words of the Gospel, &c. (*as above*).

In Masses of the Dead Cleanse my heart *is said, but the blessing is not sought, the lights are not carried, nor does the Celebrant kiss the Book.*

Then at the middle of the altar, extending, elevating, and joining his hands, he says, if it is to be said:

I believe in one God, *and he continues with joined hands. Now the Creed is said on all Sundays throughout the year, on all festivals of Christ and Mary, on the feasts of Apostles and Evangelists and Doctors of the Church, on all double feasts of the first class, &c.*

I Believe in one God (*he bows his head towards the cross*), the Father Almighty, Maker of heaven and earth, and of all things visible and invisible: And in one Lord Jesus Christ (*he bows his head to the cross*), the only-begotten Son of God, Begotten of the Father before all worlds, God of God, Light of Light, Very God of very God, Begotten not made, Consubstantial with the Father, By whom all things were made: Who for us men, and for our salvation came down from heaven: (*the passage marked with asterisks, he says kneeling*) *And was incarnate by the Holy Ghost of the Virgin Mary; and was made man,* He was crucified also for us under Pontius Pilate, He suffered and was buried, And the third day he rose again according to the Scriptures, And ascended into heaven, and sitteth on the right hand of the Father. And he shall come again with glory to judge both the quick and the dead; Whose kingdom shall have no end. And in the Holy Ghost, the Lord and giver of life, who proceedeth from the Father and the Son, who with the Father and the Son together is worshipped (*he bows his head to the cross*) and glorified, Who spake by the Prophets. And in One Holy Catholic and Apostolic Church. I acknowledge one Baptism for the remission of sins. And I look for the resurrection of the dead, And the life of the world to come. Amen. *He signs himself with the sign of the cross from the forehead to the breast.*

Then he kisses the altar, and turns to the people and says:

The Lord be with you;
℟. And with thy spirit.

Afterwards he says Let us pray *and the* Offertory, *proper to each Office.*

[*e.g. Corpus Christi.*

The Priests of the Lord do offer the offerings of the Lord made by fire and the bread of their God: therefore they shall be holy unto their God, and not profane the name of their God, Alleluia.[1]]

The Offertory having been said, if it is a Solemn Mass, the Deacon hands the Paten with the Host to the Celebrant; if private, the Priest takes the Paten with the Host, and offering it up says:

Accept, O Holy Father, Almighty and eternal God, this unspotted Host, which I, thine unworthy servant, offer unto thee, my living and true God, for my innumerable sins, offences, and negligences, and for all standing around; as also for all faithful Christians, living and departed; that it may avail both me and them for salvation unto everlasting life. Amen.

Then making the sign of the cross with the Paten, he places the Host down on the Corporal. The Deacon pours the wine, the Subdeacon the water into the Chalice, or if it is a private Mass, the Priest pours each of them, and blesses the mixed water in the Chalice ✠ *saying:*

O God, who in creating human nature, didst wonderfully dignify it, and still more wonderfully restore it, grant that, by the mystery of this water and wine, we may be made partakers of his divine nature, who vouchsafed to become partaker of our human nature, Jesus Christ thy Son, our Lord, who with thee liveth and reigneth in the unity of the Holy Ghost, world without end. Amen.

In Masses of the Dead the foregoing prayer is said, but the water is not blessed. Afterwards he takes the Chalice and offers it, saying:

We offer unto thee, O Lord, the Chalice of salvation, beseeching thy mercy: that it may ascend before thy divine Majesty as a sweet savour, for our salvation, and for that of the whole world. Amen.

[1] Adapted from Lev. 21[6]

Then he makes the sign of the cross with the Chalice and places it on the Corporal, and covers it with the Pall; then with hands joined over the altar and bowing a little he says:

In the spirit of humility and with a contrite heart may we be accepted by thee, O Lord; and may our sacrifice be so made in thy sight to-day that it may be pleasing unto thee, O Lord God.

Rising he extends his hands, and joining them held forth on high, raising his eyes towards heaven and immediately lowering them, says:

Come, O Almighty and Eternal God the Sanctifier, *he blesses the Oblations and* ble✠ss this sacrifice prepared for thy holy Name.

Afterwards, if he celebrates solemnly, he blesses the Incense, saying:

Through the intercession of blessed Michael the Archangel who standeth at the right hand of the altar of incense, and of all his elect, may the Lord vouchsafe to ble✠ss this incense, and receive it as an odour of sweetness; through Christ our Lord. Amen.

And having taken the thurible from the Deacon he censes the Oblation, saying:

May this incense which thou hast blessed, O Lord, ascend to thee, and may thy mercy descend upon us.

Then he censes the altar, saying:

Let my prayer, O Lord, be set forth in thy sight as the incense: and let the lifting up of my hands be an evening sacrifice. Set a watch, O Lord, before my mouth: and keep the door of my lips. O let not mine heart be inclined to any evil thing.

While he gives the thurible to the Deacon he says:

May the Lord kindle within us the fire of his love, and the flame of eternal charity. Amen.

Afterwards the Priest is censed by the Deacon, then the others in order.

In the meanwhile the Priest washes his hands, saying:

I will wash my hands in innocency, O Lord : and so will I go to thine altar;

That I may shew the voice of thanksgiving: and tell of all thy wondrous works.

Lord, I have loved the habitation of thy house: and the place where thine honour dwelleth.

O shut not up my soul with the sinners: nor my life with the blood-thirsty;

In whose hands is wickedness: and their right hand is full of gifts.

But as for me, I will walk innocently: O deliver me, and be merciful unto me.

My foot standeth right: I will praise the Lord in the congregations.[1]

Glory be to the Father, and to the Son, and to the Holy Ghost.

As it was in the beginning, is now, and ever shall be, world without end. Amen.

Masses of the Dead, and in Passiontide in Masses of the season the Gloria Patri *is omitted.*

Then bowing slightly in the midst of the altar, with joined hands over it, he says:

Receive, O Holy Trinity, this oblation, which we offer unto thee in memory of the Passion, Resurrection, and Ascension of our Lord Jesus Christ, and in honour of blessed Mary, ever Virgin, of blessed John the Baptist, of the holy Apostles Peter and Paul, of these and of all the Saints, that it may avail to their honour and our salvation; and may they vouchsafe to intercede for us in heaven, whose memory we celebrate on earth. Through the same Christ our Lord. Amen.

Afterwards he kisses the altar, and turns to the people; extending and joining his hands he says in an audible voice:

Pray, brethren, that my sacrifice and yours may be acceptable to God the Father Almighty.

The Minister or those standing around reply; otherwise the Priest himself:

May the Lord receive the sacrifice at thy (my) hands, to the

[1] Ps. 26[6-12].

praise and glory of his name, to our benefit, and that of all his Holy Church. *The Priest in a low voice says:* Amen.

Then with hands completely apart and without Let us pray, *he adds the* Secrets *or the* Secret, *if one is to be said.*

[*e.g.* The Ascension.

Accept, O Lord, the gifts we offer for the glorious Ascension of thy Son; and mercifully grant that we may be freed from present perils, and come to life eternal. Through the same. . . .]

The Secret Prayers being finished, when he shall have come to the end he says in an audible voice:

> The Lord be with you;
> R͘. And with thy spirit.
> Lift up your hearts;
> R͘. We lift them up unto the Lord.
> Let us give thanks unto our Lord God;
> R͘. It is meet and just.

The Preface *is recited by the Priest.*

[*e.g.* The Nativity.

It is very meet and just, right and for our salvation, that we should at all times and in all places give thanks unto thee, O holy Lord, Father Almighty, everlasting God; for through the Mystery of the Word made flesh the new light of thy glory hath shone upon the eyes of our mind: so that while we acknowledge God in visible form, we may through him be drawn to the love of things invisible. And therefore with Angels and Archangels, with the Thrones and Dominations and with all the hosts of the heavenly army we sing the hymn of thy glory evermore saying:

The Preface finished, the Priest joins his hands and bowing says: Holy, Holy, Holy Lord God of Sabaoth. Heaven and earth are full of thy glory. Hosanna in the highest.

Blessed is he that cometh in the name of the Lord. *Here he makes the sign of the cross from the forehead to the breast.*

Hosanna in the highest.]

THE CANON *begins*

Thee therefore, O most merciful Father, through Jesus Christ, thy Son our Lord, we humbly pray and entreat (*he kisses the altar*) that thou wouldest accept and bless (*he joins his hands, and then signs the Oblation thrice*) these gifts, these offerings, this ✠ holy and unspotted Sacrifice, (*then extending his hands he proceeds*) which we offer unto thee in the first place for thy Holy Catholic Church that thou wouldest be pleased to keep it in peace, to preserve, unite, and govern it throughout the world; and also for thy servant our Pope N. and our Bishop N. and all the orthodox, and those worshipping in the Catholic and Apostolic Faith.

COMMEMORATION OF THE LIVING

Remember, O Lord, thy servants and handmaidens N. and N. (*he joins his hands and prays a little for those he intends to pray for: then extending his hands he proceeds*), and all here present, whose faith is approved and whose devotion is known unto thee, for whom we offer unto thee, or who themselves offer unto thee, this Sacrifice of praise for themselves and all pertaining to them, for the redemption of their souls, for the hope of their safety and salvation; and who pay their vows to thee the eternal, living, and true God.

WITHIN THE CANON

Joining in communion with, and reverently commemorating, first the glorious and ever Virgin Mary, Mother of our God and Lord Jesus Christ; as also thy blessed Apostles and Martyrs Peter and Paul, Andrew, James, John, Thomas, James, Philip, Bartholomew, Matthew, Simon and Thaddaeus, Linus, Cletus, Clement, Sixtus, Cornelius, Cyprian, Laurence, Chrysogonus, John and Paul, Cosmas and Damian : and all thy Saints; by whose merits and prayers do thou grant that in all things we may be defended by the help of thy protection (*he joins his hands*), Through the same Christ our Lord. Amen.

[*On the Nativity, Epiphany, Resurrection, and Ascension of our Lord, again on the day of Pentecost, are inserted short introductions, e.g. The Nativity*, And celebrating this most holy day (*or* night) in which the blessed Mary immaculate Virgin brought forth a Saviour into the world,]

Holding his hands apart over the Oblation he says:

This oblation therefore of us thy servants and of thy whole family, we beseech thee, O Lord, graciously to accept; and do thou order our days in thy peace, and bid us to be delivered from eternal damnation, and to be numbered in the flock of thine elect. (*He joins his hands.*) Through Christ our Lord. Amen.

[*On the Festivals of Easter and Pentecost this prayer begins:* Which we offer unto thee for these also, whom thou hast vouchsafed to regenerate by water and the Holy Ghost, giving them remission of their sins, we beseech thee, &c.]

Which oblation do thou, Almighty God, we beseech thee, vouchsafe in all things (*he signs three times over the Oblations*) to make bles✠sed, ap✠proved, rati✠fied, reasonable, acceptable, (*he signs again over the Host and again over the Chalice*) that it may become unto us the Bo✠dy and Blo✠od of thy most dearly beloved Son, Jesus Christ our Lord.

Who the day before he suffered (*he takes the Host*) took the bread in his holy and venerable hands (*he raises his eyes to heaven*) and with eyes lifted up to heaven to thee his God and Father Almighty, giving thanks to thee, (*he signs over the Host*) he bles✠sed, brake, and gave to his disciples saying: Take, and eat ye all of this. *Holding the Host with both hands between his index fingers and thumbs, he says the words of Consecration, silently, slowly, and deliberately*: For this is my Body.

After pronouncing the words of Consecration, immediately he kneels and adores the Consecrated Host: rising, he shows it to the people, he replaces it on the Corporal, and again adores: and he does not disjoin his fingers and thumbs except when taking the Host, until after the washing of his fingers. Then uncovering the Chalice he says:

Likewise after supper (*he takes the Chalice with both hands*), taking also this excellent cup into his holy and venerable hands, also giving thanks to thee (*holding the Chalice with the left hand he signs over it with the right hand*) he bles✠sed it, and gave it to his disciples, saying: Take, and drink ye all of it. *The words of Consecration over the Chalice are said deliberately, without pausing, and holding it slightly elevated.* For this is the Cup of my Blood of the New and eternal Testament, the Mystery of Faith; which for you and for many shall be shed for remission of sins.

After the words of Consecration he replaces the Chalice on the Corporal, saying silently: As often as ye shall do these things, ye shall do them in remembrance of me.

Kneeling he adores, then rises, shows it to the people, replaces it and covers it, and again adores. Then with hands apart he says: Wherefore, O Lord, we thy servants and likewise thy holy people, mindful of the blessed passion of the same thy Son our Lord Jesus Christ, and also his resurrection from the dead, and his glorious ascension into heaven, offer unto thy most excellent Majesty of thine own gifts (*he joins his hands and signs three times the Host and Chalice together*) a pu✠re Host, a Ho✠ly Host, a spot✠less Host, (*he signs once over the Host and once over the Chalice*) Holy ✠ Bread of eternal life, and the Cup ✠ of everlasting salvation.

With hands apart he continues:

Upon which vouchsafe to look with favourable and gracious countenance, and to accept them even as thou wast pleased to accept the gifts of thy righteous servant Abel, and the sacrifice of our Patriarch Abraham, and the spotless offering which thy High Priest Melchizedek offered to thee.

Bowing down with joined hands placed upon the altar he says:

We humbly beseech thee, Almighty God, command these gifts to be borne by the hands of thy Holy Angel to thine altar on high in the sight of thy divine Majesty, that so many as (*he kisses the altar*) are partakers at the Altar (*he joins his hands and signs once over the Host and once over the Chalice*) of the Bo✠dy and Blo✠od of thy Son (*he signs himself*) may be filled with all heavenly benediction and grace. Through the same Christ our Lord Amen.

COMMEMORATION OF THE DEAD

Remember also, O Lord, the souls of thy servants N. and N., who are gone before us with the sign of faith, and rest in the sleep of peace (*he joins his hands, and prays a short while for those dead, whom he intends to pray for; then extending his hands he proceeds*), to them, O Lord, and to all that rest in Christ, grant we pray Thee, a place of refreshment, light, and peace. *He joins his hands and bows his head.* Through the same Christ our Lord. Amen.

Striking his breast with his right hand, and slightly raising his voice saying:

To us also thy sinful servants, trusting in the multitude of thy mercies, vouchsafe to grant some part and fellowship with thy holy Apostles and Martyrs, with John, Stephen, Matthias, Barnabas, Ignatius, Alexander, Marcellinus, Peter, Felicitas, Perpetua, Agatha, Lucy, Agnes, Cecilia, Anastasia, and with all thy Saints, into whose company we beseech thee to admit us, not weighing our merits but pardoning our offences (*he joins his hands*); through Christ our Lord.

By whom, O Lord, thou dost ever create (*he signs thrice over the Host and Chalice together, saying*) hal✠low, quick✠en, ble✠ss and bestow upon us all these good things, (*he uncovers the Chalice, genuflects, takes the Sacrament in his right hand, holding the Chalice in the left hand: he signs with the Host thrice from lip to lip of the Chalice, saying*) By ✠ him, and with ✠ him, and in ✠ him, be unto thee, O God the Father Al✠mighty (*he signs twice between the Chalice and his breast*), in the Unity of the Holy ✠ Ghost (*elevating slightly the Chalice with the Host he says*) All honour and glory. *He puts the Host down, covers the Chalice, genuflects, rises, and says*: World without end. ℟. Amen.

He joins his hands. Let us pray.

Admonished by saving precepts, and following divine instruction, we are bold to say: Our Father which are in heaven . . . Lead us not into temptation. ℟. But deliver us from evil.

The Priest says silently: Amen.

Then he takes the Paten between his first and second fingers and says:

Deliver us, O Lord, we beseech thee, from all evils past, present, and to come; and at the intercession of the blessed and glorious Mary ever Virgin, Mother of God, and of thy Blessed Apostles Peter and Paul and Andrew, with all Saints (*he signs himself with the Paten on his forehead, breast, and kisses it*), graciously give peace in our time, that aided by the help of thy loving kindness we may ever be set free from sin and secure from all disquietude; (*he places the Paten under the Host, uncovers the Chalice, genuflects, rises, takes the Host, breaks it through the middle over the Chalice, saying*) through the same Jesus Christ our Lord. *He places the part which is in his right hand, upon the Paten, then from the part which is in his left hand, he breaks off a Particle saying:*

Who liveth and reigneth with thee in the Unity of the Holy Ghost, God. *He places the half which is in his left hand on the Paten, and holding the Particle which he broke off in his right hand, and the Chalice in his left, says:* World without end. ℟. Amen.

With the Particle he signs thrice over the Chalice, saying:

The Peace ✠ of the Lord be ✠ alway with ✠ you;
℟. And with thy spirit.

He puts the Particle into the Chalice, saying in a low voice:

May this Commixture and Consecration of the Body and Blood of our Lord Jesus Christ avail to us that receive it unto eternal life. Amen. *He covers the Chalice, genuflects, rises, and bowing down to the Sacrament, with joined hands, and striking his breast thrice, he says:*

O Lamb of God, that takest away the sins of the world, have mercy upon us,
O Lamb of God, that takest away the sins of the world, have mercy upon us,
O Lamb of God, that takest away the sins of the world, grant us thy peace.

[*In Masses for the Dead* Have Mercy upon us *is not said, but in place of it* Grant them rest *and to the third is added* eternal.]

Then with his hands joined upon the altar, bowing down, he says:
O Lord Jesus Christ, who didst say to thine Apostles: My peace
I leave with you, my peace I give unto you: regard not my sins,
but the faith of thy church; vouchsafe to grant unto it that peace
and unity which is agreeable to thy will. Who livest and reignest,
God, world without end. Amen.

*(In Solemn Masses, where the Pax is given, the Deacon bending
the knee, with joined hands, when the prayer is finished, kisses the
altar at the same time as the Celebrant, outside the Corporal however, and receives the Pax from him, joining his left knee to the left
knee of the Celebrant. Then having first genuflected, the Caerimoni-
arius accompanying him on the left, he goes back to the choir and
distributes the Pax in that same place. In Masses for the Dead the
Pax is not given, neither is the preceding prayer said.)*

Then he says the following prayers.

O Lord Jesus Christ, Son of the living God, who by the will
of the Father and the co-operation of the Holy Ghost hast by
thy death given life to the world; deliver me by this thy most holy
Body and Blood, from all my iniquities and from every evil: and
make me always to cleave to thy commandments, and suffer me
not to be ever separated from thee. Who with the same God
the Father and the Holy Ghost, livest and reignest God, World
without end. R̶. Amen.

Let not the partaking of thy Body and Blood, O Lord Jesus
Christ, which I, though unworthy, presume to receive, turn to
my judgement and condemnation; but let it through thy mercy
become a means of defence and healing, both of body and soul;
who with God the Father in the Unity of the Holy Ghost, livest
and reignest, God, world without end. Amen.

He genuflects, rises, and says:

I will take the Bread of heaven, and will call upon the name of
the Lord.

*Then slightly inclining, he takes both the parts of the Host between
the thumb and index finger of his left hand, and the Paten between
the same forefinger and the middle one, and with his right hand*

striking his breast, and slightly raising his voice, he says thrice devoutly aud humbly:

Lord, I am not worthy that thou shouldest come under my roof, but speak the word only, and my soul shall be healed.

Afterwards, signing himself with his right hand with the Host over the Paten, he says:

The Body of our Lord Jesus Christ preserve my soul unto eternal life. Amen.

He reverently receives both halves of the Host, joins his hands, and meditates for a short while on the Holy Sacrament. Then he uncovers the Chalice, genuflects, collects any fragments which may be [on the Corporal], wipes the Paten over the Chalice, saying in the meanwhile: What return shall I make to the Lord for all he has given to me? I will take the cup of salvation and will call upon the name of the Lord. Praising I will call upon the Lord, and I shall be saved from my enemies.

He takes the Chalice in his right hand, and signing himself with it says:

The Blood of our Lord Jesus Christ preserve my soul unto eternal life. Amen.

He receives all the Blood together with the Particle. If there are any to be communicated in the Mass (this is what the Church desires), the Priest after receiving the Blood, before he washes his fingers, makes a genuflexion and puts the consecrated particles into the Pyx or, if there are only a few to be communicated, on to the Paten, unless they have been placed in the Pyx or another Chalice from the beginning. In the meanwhile the Minister holds out a linen veil, or a white covering, in front of them, and makes the Confession for them, saying: I confess, &c., *as above. Then the Priest again genuflects, and with joined hands turning himself to the people at the Gospel side says:* May Almighty God have mercy upon you, forgive you your sins, and bring you to everlasting life. *And* May the Almighty and merciful Lord grant unto you pardon, absolution, and remission of your sins. *And with his right hand he makes the sign of the cross over them. Afterwards genuflecting he takes with his left hand the*

*Pyx or Paten with the Sacrament, but takes with the right hand one
Particle, which he holds between his thumb and forefinger elevated
a little over the Pyx or Paten, and turning to the Communicants at
the middle of the altar, he says:*

Behold the Lamb of God, that taketh away the sins of the world.

Then he says:

Lord, I am not worthy that thou shouldest come under my
roof, but speak the word only, and my soul shall be healed. *Which
words are repeated three times; he then goes to their right side, i.e.
the Epistle side, and administers the Sacrament to each one, making
with it the sign of the cross over the Pyx or Paten and at the same
time saying:*

The Body of our Lord Jesus Christ preserve thy soul unto everlasting life.

*When all have communicated he returns to the altar, saying
nothing, and does not give a blessing, because he will give that at the
end of the Mass. If Particles were placed on the Corporal, he wipes
it together with the Paten, and if any have been on it he drops the
fragments into the Chalice.*

Afterwards he says:

Grant, O Lord, that what we have taken with our mouth, we
may retain with a pure mind and that from a temporal gift it
may become to us an eternal remedy.

*In the meanwhile he holds out the Chalice to the Minister, who
pours into it a little wine, with which he purifies it; then he continues:*

May thy Body, O Lord, which I have received, and thy Blood,
which I have drunk, cleave to my inmost heart; and grant that
no stain of sin may remain in me, who have been fed with pure
and holy Sacraments, Who livest and reignest world without
end. Amen.

*He washes his fingers, wipes them, and consumes the ablutions;
he wipes his mouth and the Chalice, which he covers, and having
folded the Corporal, places it on the altar as at the beginning. Then*

at the Epistle side he reads the Antiphon, which is called the Communion, *and varies with the Office.*

[*e.g. Third Mass of Christmas Day.*

All the ends of the world have seen the salvation of our God.[1]]

With hands joined before his breast he goes to the middle of the altar, and having kissed it he turns himself to the people and says:

The Lord be with you;

R̷. And with thy spirit.

He returns to the Book and says a prayer, which is called Post-Communion, *one or more as the Office requires.*

[*e.g. Third Mass of Christmas Day.*

Grant, we beseech thee, Almighty God, that as the Saviour of the world, born on this day, is the author of our heavenly birth, so he may also be to us the giver of immortality. Who with thee . . .]

Which being finished he closes the Book and joining his hands before his breast he returns to the middle of the altar, where having kissed it he turns to the people saying:

The Lord be with you;

R̷. And with thy spirit.

Then he says, if it is to be said:

Go, the Mass is finished. *In Easter-tide* Alleluia *is added.*

[*But if it is not to be said, as during Advent and Lent, &c., having said* The Lord be with you, *standing facing the altar he says:* Let us bless the Lord. *In Masses of the Dead:* May they rest in peace.

In the Lenten Office another prayer comes after the Post-Communion prayer, Over the people, *after* Let us pray. Bow down your heads to God, *has first been said. Then* The Lord be with you *as above.*]

Go, the Mass is finished, *or* Let us bless the Lord, *having been said, the Priest bows down before the midst of the altar, and with hands joined over it says:*

May the performance of my service be pleasing unto thee, O Holy Trinity, and grant that the sacrifice, which I, unworthy,

<hr />

[1] Ps. 98. Part of v. 4.

have offered in the sight of thy Majesty, may be acceptable to thee, and through thy mercy may be a propitiation for me and for those for whom I have offered it. Through Christ our Lord. Amen.

Then he kisses the altar and having raised his eyes, extending, lifting up, and joining his hands and bowing his head to the cross, says:

May Almighty God bless you, *and turning to the people, blessing once only, even in Solemn Masses, he continues:*

Father and Son ✠ and Holy Ghost.
R̷. Amen.

In Pontifical Masses the Blessing is given three times.

Then at the Gospel side is said: The Lord be with you. R̷. And with thy spirit, *signing the altar or the Book and himself, as above at the Gospel of the Mass, he reads* The Gospel according to St. John 1^{1-14}. In the beginning was the Word. *When he says* And the Word was made flesh *he kneels. At the conclusion* Thanks be to God *is the response.*

[*If another festival of superior rank should fall during the Lenten fast and the four Ember seasons, on Vigils and Sundays, the Mass of the Feast is read, but the Gospel of the Day is read at the finish. In the Third Mass of Christmas the Gospel of the Epiphany is used:* When Jesus was born.

In Masses of the Dead the Blessing is not given, but having said May they rest in peace *he says* May the performance of, &c. *Then having kissed the altar he reads the Gospel of St. John. Descending from the altar for the Thanksgiving he says the Song of the Three Children and several collects.*]

D

II. THE AMBROSIAN RITE

A private prayer is said before the Priest goes to the altar: and again another when he comes there, e.g. Psalm Be merciful unto me, O God. *Standing on the lowest step of the altar he signs himself with the sign of the cross and says alternately with the Ministers the following Psalm.*

Give sentence with me, O God. Ps. 43.
Glory be to the Father, &c.
P. O give thanks unto the Lord, for he is gracious;
M. For his mercy endureth for ever.[1]

I confess to God Almighty, to blessed Mary ever virgin, to blessed Michael the Archangel, to blessed John the Baptist, to the holy Apostles Peter and Paul, to all the saints, and to you, brethren, that I have sinned exceedingly, in thought, word, and deed, through my fault, my fault, my most grievous fault. Wherefore I pray blessed Mary, blessed Michael the Archangel, blessed John the Baptist, the holy Apostles Peter and Paul, all the saints, and you, brethren, to pray for me to the Lord our God.

The Ministers reply:

May Almighty God have mercy upon thee, forgive thee thy sins, and bring thee to everlasting life.
P. Amen.

Then the Ministers repeat the Confession:

P. May the Almighty God have mercy upon you, forgive you your sins, and bring you to everlasting life. ℞. Amen.
P. May the Almighty and merciful Lord grant us pardon, absolution, and remission of our sins. ℞. Amen.
P. Our help standeth in the Name of the Lord;[2]
℞. Who hath made heaven and earth.
P. Blessed be the Name of the Lord;[3]
℞. From this time forth and for evermore.

---

[1] Ps. 107[1].   [2] Ps. 124[7].   [3] Ps. 113[2].

He says silently:

I entreat thee, O most high God of Saboath, Holy Father, that I may be able to intercede for my sins, and for those present to gain pardon of their sins, and to offer a peace offering for each one. Through Christ our Lord. Amen.

Going up to the altar he says:

We pray thee, O Lord, through the merits of thy Saints, whose relics are here, and of all the saints, that thou wouldest vouchsafe to forgive me all my sins. Amen.

Then he reads the Ingressa, *which in the Roman rite is called the Introit, but without the Psalm, and without repetition and without* Glory be, &c.

[*e.g. First Sunday in Advent.*

Unto Thee, O Lord, will I lift up my soul; my God, I have put my trust in thee: O let me not be confounded, neither let mine enemies triumph over me. For all they that hope in thee shall not be ashamed.[1]]

The Ingressa *being finished he says*, The Lord be with you, *not turning himself to the people.*

℞. And with thy spirit.

There follows the Prayer over the people, *one or more as is appointed for the day. They are always an uneven number, not exceeding nine; each collection[2] has four prayers, namely, over the People, over the Linen Cloth, over the Oblation, and the Post-Communion.*

Then follows Glory be to God on High, &c. *if it is to be said, as in the Roman rite.*

Then Kyrie eleison, Kyrie eleison, Kyrie eleison.

Then follows the Prophetic Lection. *Once it was assigned to all Masses, but now only to Masses of Lent, of the most holy Sacrament,*

---

[1] Ps. 25[1].

[2] *Collecta* = 'The assembling of the people for divine worship' Probably it refers here to the fact that each Mass has four such collects as mentioned in the text.

and to Masses after Pentecost. In the feasts of Easter, Ascension, and Pentecost, the Lection is read from the Acts of the Apostles.

[*e.g. Advent I it is*: Isaiah 51^{1-8}.

Hearken to me . . . generation to generation.]

Then follows the Psalmulus [*a verse and response almost always from the Psalms*].

The Lord be with you;
℟. And with thy spirit.

Silence is proclaimed.

The Epistle *is read.*

[*e.g. Advent I*, 2 Thess. 2^{1-14}.

Now we beseech you . . . patient toward all men.]

After the Epistle there follows the Alleluia *and* Verse, *or a chant without Alleluia, according to the season.*

The Lord be with you;
℟. And with thy spirit.

The Deacon, signing himself on the forehead, mouth, and breast, says:

The Lection of the Holy Gospel according to N.
℟. Glory be to thee, O Lord.

Then inclining towards the cross he asks a blessing, which is similar to the Roman: then he reads the Gospel.

The Gospel being finished the Priest says:

The Lord be with you;
℟. And with thy spirit.

Kyrie eleison, Kyrie eleison, Kyrie eleison.

The Lord be with you;
℟. And with thy spirit.

And the Antiphon after the Gospel *is said, proper to each Office.* [*Almost always from the Psalms.*]

Have ye peace;
℟. With thee, Lord.

The Lord be with you;
℟. And with thy spirit.

Then is said aloud the Prayer over the Sindon, i.e. the Linen Cloth, with which the altar is covered.

Now is made [at least in the Cathedral Church of Milan] from an old custom the Oblation of bread and wine. [Cf. Muratorii Antiquit. Ital. m. a., t. iv, p. 854.]

The Celebrant receives the Paten with the Host and offers it, saying:

Accept, most merciful Father, this holy bread, that it may become the Body of thy Only-begotten One, in the name of the Father, and of the Son, and of the Holy Ghost. Amen.

Then he pours water into the Chalice, saying:

From the side of Christ came forth blood and water together. In the name of the Father, and of the Son, and of the Holy Ghost. Amen.

Then he offers the Chalice, saying:

Accept, O Holy Trinity, this Chalice, wine and water mixed, that it may become the Blood of thy Only-begotten One. In the name of the Father, and of the Son, and of the Holy Ghost. Amen.

Then with joined hands and bowing he says:

O Almighty and Everlasting God, may this oblation be pleasing and acceptable to thee, which I unworthy offer to thy Godliness for myself a wretched sinner and for my innumerable faults, that thou wouldest grant me pardon and remission of my sins, and shalt not have despised my iniquities, but thy mercy alone may be profitable to me though unworthy.

Then standing with extended hands he proceeds:

And accept, O Holy Trinity, this oblation, which we offer unto thee, for the government and custody and unity of the catholic faith and for the veneration of the Blessed Mary Mother of God and also of all thy Saints, and for the salvation and safety of thy servants and handmaids and of all those for whom we have promised to implore thy mercy and of those whose alms we have received; and of all faithful Christians living and departed: that through thy mercy they may obtain remission of all their sins, and continuing faithfully in thy praises may deserve the reward of eternal happiness, to the glory and honour of thy name, O God, most merciful author of all things. Through Christ our Lord.

On Sundays and on feasts of Saints he says another Prayer of similar content.

Then holding his hands apart over the Oblation he says:

Receive, O Holy Trinity, this oblation for my cleansing, that thou mayest cleanse and purge me from all stains of sins, so that I may be meet to minister worthily unto thee, O God and most Merciful Lord.

Afterwards he blesses the Oblation with these words:

The Blessing of God Almighty the Father and the Son and the Holy Ghost come down abundantly from heaven on this our oblation and may this oblation be acceptable to thee, Holy Lord, Father Almighty, Eternal God, most merciful author of all things. Amen.

The Offerenda *or* Offertory *is sung.*

In the meanwhile the Priest censes the altar and the Oblations, saying:

Let my prayer be set forth in thy sight, as the incense: and let the lifting up of my hands be an evening sacrifice. [*As in the Roman Ordo.*][1]

When he hands back the thurible to the Deacon he says:

Behold the odour of the Saints of God is as the odour of a full field, which the Lord hath blessed.[2]

The Lord be with you;
R̷. And with thy spirit.

[1] Ps. 141[2, 3, 4].
[2] Founded on Gen. 27[27].

Now is said the Creed, *if it is said, chiefly on Sundays and festivals.*

The Lord be with you;
R̷. And with thy spirit.

He says in a loud voice one or more Prayers over the Oblations [*like the Roman Secrets*].

[*e.g. The Ascension.*

O Lord, we now most humbly offer the Sacrifice for the Ascension of thy venerable Son; Grant, we beseech thee, that we through him by these most holy gifts[1] may rise to the heavenlies. Through Christ our Lord.]

Then he says:

The Lord be with you;
R̷. And with thy spirit.
Lift up your hearts;
R̷. We lift them up unto the Lord.
Let us give thanks unto our Lord God;
R̷. It is meet and just.

The Preface follows, proper to each feast and ferial. [*The Ambrosian Preface for the Nativity is the same as the Roman. We give another for third after Easter.*]

It is very meet, and just, right and for our salvation that we should at all times and in all places give thanks unto Thee, O Holy Lord, Father Almighty, everlasting God. Through Christ, our Lord; Who pitying human error, vouchsafed to be born of a Virgin; and by the passion of death delivered us from eternal death, and by His resurrection hath bestowed eternal life on us; the same Jesus Christ, our Lord. Whom together with thee, &c.

Holy, Holy, Holy, Lord God of Sabaoth.
Heaven and earth are full of thy glory.
Hosanna in the highest.

Blessed is he that cometh in the name of the Lord
Hosanna in the highest.

[1] *Commercium,* lit. Commercial intercourse.

THE CANON *begins*

Thee therefore, O most merciful Father, through Jesus Christ, thy Son our Lord, we humbly pray and entreat, that thou wouldest accept and bless these gifts, these offerings, this holy and unspotted Sacrifice, which we offer unto thee in the first place for thy Holy Catholic Church, that thou wouldest be pleased to keep it in peace, to preserve, unite and govern it throughout the world; and also for thy servant our Pontiff N., thy servant N., our emperor, and all the orthodox, and those worshipping in the Catholic and Apostolic Faith.

COMMEMORATION OF THE LIVING

Remember, O Lord, thy servants and handmaidens N. and N., and all here present, whose faith is approved and whose devotion is known unto thee, for whom we offer unto thee, or who themselves offer unto thee, this Sacrifice of praise for themselves and all pertaining to them, for the redemption of their souls, for the hope of their safety and salvation; and who pay their vows to thee the eternal, living, and true God.

WITHIN THE CANON

Joining in communion with, and reverently commemorating, first the glorious and ever Virgin Mary, Mother of our God and Lord Jesus Christ; as also thy blessed Apostles and Martyrs Peter and Paul, Andrew, James, John, Thomas, James, Philip, Bartholomew, Matthew, Simon and Thaddaeus : Sixtus, Laurence, Hippolytus, Vincent, Cornelius, Cyprian, Clement, Chrysogonas, John and Paul, Cosmas and Damian, Apollinarius, Vitalian, Nazarius and Celsus, Protase and Gervase, and all thy Saints; by whose merits and prayers do thou grant that in all things we may be defended by the help of thy protection. Through the same Christ our Lord.

[*On the Nativity, Epiphany, Resurrection, and Ascension of our Lord, again on the day of Pentecost, are inserted short introductions, e.g. the Nativity,* And celebrating this most holy day (*or* night) in which the blessed Mary immaculate Virgin brought forth a saviour into the world,]

This oblation therefore of us thy servants and of thy whole family, we beseech thee, O Lord, graciously to accept; and do thou order our days in thy peace, and bid us to be delivered from eternal damnation, and to be numbered in the flock of thine elect. Through Christ our Lord. Amen.

Which oblation which we offer to thy goodness do thou, O God, we beseech thee, vouchsafe in all things to make bles✠sed, ap✠proved, rati✠fied, reasonable, acceptable, that it may become unto us the Bo✠dy and Blo✠od of thy most dearly beloved Son Jesus Christ our Lord.

Here he cleanses his consecrated fingers.

Who the day before he suffered taking bread in his holy and venerable hands and with eyes lifted up to heaven to thee his God and Father Almighty, giving thanks to thee, he blessed, brake, and gave to his disciples saying: Take, and eat ye all of this. For this is my Body [*or as in the text of Pamelius:* This is my Body which is broken for you].

Likewise after supper, taking also this excellent cup into his holy and venerable hands, also giving thanks to thee, he blessed it, and gave it to his disciples, saying: Take, and drink ye all of it. For this is the Cup of my Blood of the New and eternal Testament, the Mystery of Faith; which for you and for many, shall be shed for remission of sins [*or in the text of Pamelius:* This is my Blood]. *He makes the elevation:* Commanding also and saying to them: As often as ye shall do this, ye shall do it in memory of me, ye shall shew forth my death, ye shall announce my resurrection, ye shall hope for my advent, until I come again from heaven to you.

Wherefore, O Lord, we thy servants and likewise thy holy people, mindful of the blessed passion of the same thy Son our Lord Jesus Christ, and also his resurrection from the dead, and his glorious ascension into heaven, offer unto thy most excellent Majesty of thine own gifts a pure Host, a Holy Host, a spotless Host, Holy Bread of eternal life, and the Cup of everlasting salvation.

Upon which vouchsafe to look with favourable and gracious countenance, and to accept them even as thou wast pleased to accept the gifts of thy righteous servant Abel, and the sacrifice of our patriarch Abraham, and the spotless offering which thy High Priest Melchizedek offered to thee.

We humbly beseech thee, Almighty God, command these gifts to be borne by the hands of thy holy Angel to thine Altar on high in the sight of thy divine Majesty, that so many as are partakers at the Altar of the Body and Blood of thy Son may be filled with all heavenly benediction and grace. Through the same Christ our Lord.

Remember also, O Lord, the souls of thy servants N. and N., who are gone before us with the sign of faith, and rest in the sleep of peace, to them, O Lord, and to all that rest in Christ, grant, we pray thee, a place of refreshment, light, and peace. Through the same Christ our Lord.

To us also thy sinful servants, trusting in the multitude of thy mercies, vouchsafe to grant some part and fellowship with thy holy Apostles and Martyrs, with John, Stephen, and Andrew, Peter, Marcellinus, Agnes, Cecilia, Felicitas, Perpetua, Anastasia, Agatha, Euphemia, Lucy, Apollonius, Justin, Sabina, Thecla, Pelagius, and Catherine, and with all thy Saints, into whose company we beseech thee to admit us, not weighing our merits but pardoning our offences, through Christ our Lord.

By whom, O Lord, thou dost ever create, hallow, quicken and bless and abundantly bestow upon us thy servants, to the increase of our faith and remission of all our sins. From him, and by him, and in him, be unto thee, O God the Father Almighty in the Unity of the Holy Ghost, all honour, power, praise, glory, empire, perpetuity and power, through infinity world without end. Amen.

He breaks the Host into two portions, saying: Thy Body is broken, O Christ, the Cup is blessed. *He breaks the other portion again, and says:* Thy Blood be always unto us for the life and for the salvation of our souls, O our God. *Then putting the*

Particle into the Chalice, he says: May the Commixture of the consecrated Body and Blood of our Lord Jesus Christ be to us who eat and receive for profit unto life and joy everlasting.

In the meanwhile the Antiphon is sung varying with the Office of the day, which is called Confractorium. *And immediately he says:*[1]

Let us pray.

Admonished by saving precepts, and following divine instruction, we are bold to say:

Our Father . . . lead us not into temptation;

R̂. But deliver us from evil.

The Priest says: Amen.

He says in a loud voice:

Deliver us, O Lord, we beseech thee, from all evils past, present, and to come; and at the intercession of the blessed and glorious Mary ever Virgin, Mother of God, and of thy blessed Apostles Peter and Paul and Andrew, and blessed Ambrose thy Confessor and Pontiff, and all thy Saints, graciously give peace in our time, that aided by the help of thy loving kindness we may be ever set free from sin and secure from all disquietude; Through the same Jesus Christ our Lord, thy Son. Who liveth and reigneth with thee in the Unity of the Holy Ghost, God. World without end.

The Peace and Fellowship of our Lord Jesus Christ be ever with you;

R̂. And with thy Spirit.

Shew the Peace among yourselves.

R̂. Thanks be to God.

(O Lamb of God *is said only in Masses for the Dead.*)

O Lord, Jesu Christ, who didst say to thine Apostles: My peace I leave with you, my peace I give unto you: regard not my sins, but the faith of thy church; vouchsafe to grant unto it that peace and unity which is agreeable to thy will. Who livest and reignest, God, world without end. Amen.

[1] *Subdit*, i.e. puts near or applies.

O Lord Jesu Christ, Son of the living God, who by the will of the Father and the co-operation of the Holy Ghost hast by thy death given life to the world; deliver me by this thy most holy Body and Blood, from all my iniquities and from every evil: and make me always to cleave to thy commandments, and suffer me not to be ever separated from thee; Who with the same God the Father and the Holy Ghost, livest and reignest God, world without end. Amen.

Let not the partaking of thy Body and Blood, O Lord Jesu Christ, which I, though unworthy, presume to receive, turn to my judgement and condemnation; but let it, through thy Mercy, become a means of defence and healing, both of body and soul; who with God the Father in the Unity of the Holy Ghost, livest and reignest, God, world without end. Amen.

I will take the Bread of heaven and will call upon the name of the Lord.

Lord, I am not worthy that thou shouldest come under my roof, but speak the word only and my soul shall be healed.

May the Body of our Lord Jesus Christ profit me who receive it, and to all for whom I have offered this sacrifice, unto life and joy everlasting.

What return shall I make to the Lord for all he has given to me? I will receive the cup of salvation and will call upon the name of the Lord. Praising I will call upon the Lord, and I shall be saved from my enemies.

Thanks be to God, thanks be to God, we take the accepted gift of Christ the grace of God not for our judgement but for the salvation of our souls, O our God. O Lamb of God, that takest away the sins of the world, have mercy upon us. Glory be to the Father, and to the Son, and to the Holy Ghost. As it was in the beginning, is now, and ever shall be, world without end. O Lamb of God, that takest away the sins of the world, have mercy upon us. Receive our prayer; who sittest at the right hand of the Father. O Lamb of God, that takest away the sins of the world, grant us thy peace.

Among the Ambrosians is said by the Priest who administers the Sacrament:

The Body of Christ.
Amen *is responded.*

He says at the Epistle side the Antiphon, which is called Transitorium.

[*e.g. Epiphany VI.*

Turn ye, O ye sons of men, while ye have time, saith the Lord; and I will write your names in the book of my Father which is in heaven.[1]]

The Lord be with you;
R̶. And with thy spirit.

The Post-Communion *follows.*

The Lord be with you;
R̶. And with thy spirit.

Kyrie eleison, Kyrie eleison, Kyrie eleison.

In the middle of the altar he signs himself, saying:

God bless us and hear us;
R̶. Amen.
Let us go forth in peace;
R̶. In the name of Christ.
Let us bless the Lord;
R̶. Thanks be to God.

The Priest says:

May the performance of my service be pleasing unto thee, O Holy Trinity; grant that the sacrifice, which I, unworthy, have offered in the sight of thy Majesty, may be acceptable to thee, and through thy mercy may be a propitiation for me, and for those for whom I have offered it. Through Christ our Lord. Amen.

He blesses the people after this manner:

May the divine Majesty, the Father ✠ and the Holy Ghost ✠ bless you;
R̶. Amen.

[1] Not from Scripture, but probably composed for the occasion.

[*In festivals of Saints the name of the Saint is added, e.g. S. Ambrose:*

By the prayers and merits of Blessed Pontiff and confessor Ambrose, God bless ✠ you and bring you to the joy of paradise; ℟. Amen.]

Then he reads the beginning of the Gospel according to S. John.

Going back he says the Song of the Three Children.

III. THE GALLICAN LITURGY

The Antiphon *with* Glory be to the Father, &c., *is sung.*

The Deacon proclaims silence. The Priest says:

The Lord be ever with you;

℟. And with thy spirit.

The Trisagion *is sung in Greek and Latin. Three boys sing together. (Ore uno.)*[1]

Kyrie eleison, Christe eleison, Kyrie eleison, &c.

The Canticle of Zacharias. [*This is the 'Benedictus' and is called the* Prophecy. *It is chanted alternately. In later times the Roman custom was adopted of singing the* Gloria.]

THE COLLECT AFTER THE PROPHECY

[*A variable prayer, e.g. The Nativity.*[2]

Thou art risen unto us, O true Sun of righteousness, Jesus Christ, thou hast come from heaven the saviour of the human race; thou hast raised up a horn of salvation for us, and of an exalted parentage the everlasting offspring, begotten in the house of David according to the oracle of the ancient prophets; desiring to deliver thine own people and to destroy the 'writing' (chirographum) of old sins, that thou mightest extend the triumph of eternal life. And therefore we now beseech thee, that in the bowels of thy tender mercy thou wouldest appear to our souls, O Eternal Saviour; and in delivering us from the evil enemy thou wouldest make us worshippers of righteousness; and that we having put away every mortal error and walking directly in the way of peace, may be able to serve thee rightly, O Saviour of the world, who with the Father and the Holy Ghost liveth and ruleth and reigneth, God, world without end.]

The Prophetic Lection. (*A lesson read from the Old Testament, or if a Saint's day a lection of the passion, or of the life of the Saint.*) [*e.g. the Bobbio Missal for the Daily Mass gives* Daniel 12[1-3].]

[1] See Le Brun, vol. ii, p. 251, ed. 1726.

[2] *Missale Gothicum,* Henry Bradshaw Society.

The Psalmus responsorius. [*This corresponds to the 'Psallendo' of the Mozarabic rite, and the 'Psalmulus' of the Ambrosian. It consisted of a few verses of a Psalm, one verse being sung by a cantor, and the next by the people as it were responding.*][1]

The Deacon: Make silence.

Then follows the Epistle. [*In the Bobbio Missal the Epistle for daily use is* 2 Cor. 10[17]–11[2] *and begins* Brethren . . .]

The Deacon proceeds to the Ambo to read the Gospel. *At the beginning the clerks respond:*

Glory be to thee, O Lord.

and at the end, Glory be to God Almighty.

While the Deacon is returning from the Ambo Sanctus *is sung.*[2]

Then follow the Homily, *the* Litany, *and the* Collect after the Litany.

[*For an example of a Litany see* Stowe Missal, *p.* 75.]

COLLECT AFTER THE LITANY

[*e.g. The Nativity.*[3]

Hear, O Lord, a family devoted unto thee and gathered together in the bosom of thy Church on this solemn day of thy Nativity in order that it may proclaim thy praises. Grant redemption to the captives, sight to the blind, remission to sinners, for thou camest in order to save us. Behold from thy holy heaven, and illuminate thy people whose soul with a full devotion trusts in thee, O Saviour of the world, who liveth, &c.]

(*The Catechumens and those who are not worthy to remain go out.*)

Silence is proclaimed.

The Preface of the Mass *and the* Collect before the Names *are said.*

[1] Mabillon, *De Lit. Gall.*, p. 38.
[2] Duchesne, *Christian Worship*, p. 197.
[3] *Missale Gothicum*, H.B.S.

THE PREFACE

[*e.g. In the* Missale Gothicum, *Sunday Mass V.*[1]

O God, who by governing us preservest us, by sparing us makest us righteous, both deliver us in temporal tribulation, and bestow upon us eternal joys. Through, &c.

THE COLLECT BEFORE THE NAMES

O God, the merciful teacher of those who hope in thee, absolve us from all participation of wickedness, neither suffer us to be drawn from any chains of iniquities that from whence is our whole goodness, from thence may be our safe freedom. Through our Lord.]

Sonum. [*This is an Antiphon corresponding to the Roman Offertory.*]

The Oblation *of the gifts is made. (The Deacon or one of the Sacred Ministers brings in the previously prepared Oblations. The Priest, after that he has satisfied himself that sufficient bread and wine have been prepared, pours a little water into the Chalice and covers it with a pall or veil.)*[2]

Having arranged the Oblation on the altar he says:

Come, O Almighty and eternal God, the Sanctifier, and bless this sacrifice prepared for thy name. Through Christ our Lord.

The Diptychs *are read after the Oblation,*[3] *that is to say, the names are recited of those Saints in whose memory the sacrifice is offered to God, then of the living, and also of the departed, for whom it is offered. [The form of these Diptychs is preserved for us at the end of the 'Rule of Aurelian', one-time Bishop of Arles.]*

And praying together we pray also, O Lord, for the souls of thy servants, and also our former Fathers and instructors, Aurelian, Peter, Florentinus, Redemptius, Constantine, Himiterus, Hilary, Januarius, Reparatus, Childebertius, Voltrogota, and of all our brethren whom thou hast deigned to call from this place to thee. And also we are mindful of all the faithful of this place,

---

[1] *Missale Gothicum*, H.B.S. [2] See Mabillon, op. cit., pp. 39 ff.
[3] Ibid., p. 43.

as well as our parents and worshippers of this place; and for the souls of all thy faithful servants and handmaidens, and strangers departed in the peace of the Church, that thou, O Lord our God, wouldest grant unto them pardon of their sins and bestow upon them rest eternal. By the merits and intercessions of thy Saints, Mary, Mother of our Lord Jesus Christ, Stephen, Peter, Paul, John, James, Andrew, Philip, Thomas, Bartholomew, Matthew, James, Simon, Judas, Matthias, Genesius, Symphorian, Bandilius, Victor, Hilary bishop and confessor, Martin bishop and confessor, Caesarius bishop, do thou favourably vouchsafe to grant these things and to hearken; Who livest and reignest in the Unity of the Holy Ghost, God, world without end. Amen.

THE COLLECT AFTER THE NAMES

[*e.g. Bobbio Missal, Daily Mass.*

Sanctify, O Lord, the gifts offered; and cleanse us from the stains of our sins.

THE COLLECT FOR PEACE[1]

e.g. Bobbio Missal as above.

May this oblation of thy people be pleasing unto thee, O Lord, which we offer to thee in honour of thy name; may it be profitable to all for salvation.]

Contestatio, *or* Illatio *or* Immolatio. [*This corresponds to the Preface of the Roman rite. If the Mass is for a Saint the Contestatio contains the recitation of incidents in the life of the Saint.*[2]]

[*The Gallican Prefaces were usually long. Two examples are given in Linton's* Twenty Five Consecration Prayers, *S.P.C.K., 1921, pp. 110 ff. Here is given the Preface in daily use from the Bobbio Missal.*]

It is very meet and just, right and for our salvation that we should at all times and in all places give thanks unto thee, O Lord, Holy Father, Almighty everlasting God. Through Christ our Lord, through whom the angels praise thy Majesty, the

---

[1] This prayer accompanied the Kiss of Peace.
[2] Mabillon, p. 45.

Dominions adore, the Powers tremble, the heavens and the heavenly host, and the blessed seraphim in triumphant chorus, unite to celebrate. With whom we entreat thee that thou wouldest permit our voices to be admitted, while we say with humble praise:

Holy, holy, holy *is sung*.

THE CANON *begins*

The Priest recites the Post-Sanctus Collect, *a brief prayer which varies with the Mass.*

[*e.g. The Vigil of the Nativity.*

Truly holy, truly blessed is our Lord Jesus Christ thy Son, abiding in the heavens, was manifested on the earth. For he himself the day before he suffered, &c.]

[*These are the first words of the sacred Canon or Consecration. In the* Missale Francorum *the Gregorian Canon is assigned, and in the Bobbio Missal the Roman Canon is given.*]

For he himself the day before he suffered, &c.

[*In the four Gallican Missals which exist, the remainder of the words are missing. It is certain from the writings of SS. Germain and Gregory of Tours that the Catholic custom was to bless the sacred gifts by making the sign of the cross, and to pronounce the sacred words over them; which were said in this manner, or in a very similar form:*]

This ✠ is my Body, which is broken for you.

This ✠ is the Cup of my Blood, the Mystery of Faith; which for you and for many shall be shed for remission of sins.

The Collect *after the* Mystery *or the* Post-Secreta *is said. This prayer also varies with the Mass.*

[*e.g. The Nativity.*[1]

O Lord, we believe in thine advent; we recollect thy passion; thy Body was broken in remission of our sins, thy holy Blood was poured out as the price of our redemption; Who with the Father and the Holy Ghost liveth and reigneth world without end.]

[1] *Missale Gothicum*, H.B.S.

The Fraction *and the* Commixture *are made while the clerks humbly sing an Antiphon.*

The Lord's Prayer is prefaced with a variable formula.

[*e.g. The Nativity.*[1]

Not presuming by our merits, Holy Father, but obeying the command of our Lord Jesus Christ, we are bold to say:]
Our Father . . .[2]

The embolismos also varied with the Mass.

[*e.g. The Nativity.*

Deliver us, Almighty God, from every evil, and guard us in every good work, perfect truth and true freedom, O God, who reignest world without end.[3]]

[*The* Benediction *preceded the Communion. It was given by the Bishop or the Priest; usually in the triple form, as in the Mozarabic rite, but not always, as the following example from those published by Thomasius. This is for S. Andrew.*]

Lord God Almighty, who sitting above the stars in thy glory, has left unto us a favourable star, blessed Apostles, whose fair attendants, mighty in blessed splendour, thou didst elect first in merit, that thou mightest predestinate them in the kingdom.
R̷. Amen.
Of thy mercy grant to those standing around to be strengthened with the sign of the cross, that it may overcome every attack of the evil power.
R̷. Amen.
Pour into their minds the apostolic teaching, that they may contemplate thee with clear minds.
R̷. Amen.
That in the great hour of judgement they may be defended by the protection of those whose precepts they have followed.
R̷. Amen.

---

[1] *Missale Gothicum*, H.B.S.   [2] Mabillon, p. 49.
[3] Cp. *Book of Deer*, Dimma, Mulling.

Which vouchsafe to grant, who with the Father and with the Holy Ghost liveth and reigneth God, world without end.

℟. Amen.

After the Benediction and the Priest's Communion, the Faithful who are to communicate go up to the altar, the women also. When they have received the Eucharistic Particle, the Chalice is administered by the Deacon.

The Trecanum. [*This is an Antiphon which was sung during the Communion. It is mentioned by S. Germain, and according to him it had some relation to the Mystery of the Trinity.*[1]]

[*In the Gallican books two prayers are mentioned after the Communion. The first is called the* Post-Communion Collect *and the other the* Consummation of the Mass, *or* For the People. *Both prayers varied with the Mass; those given here are from the Bobbio Missal for the Daily Mass.*]

POST-COMMUNION

Grant, O Lord, we beseech thee, that we whom thou hast fed with heavenly food, may be cleansed from our secret sins, and delivered from the snares of our enemies.

THE CONSUMMATION OF THE MASS

We give thanks unto thee, O Lord, Holy Father, Almighty everlasting God, who hast fed us with the Communion of the Body and Blood of Christ thy Son; and we humbly implore thy mercy, that this thy sacrament, O Lord, may not be a condemnation to us, but a wholesome intercession for pardon, may be a cleansing of sins, strength of the weak, may be a means of strength against the dangers of the world. May this Communion, O Lord, cleanse us from sin and allow us to be partakers of the heavenly joys. Through Christ our Lord. Amen.

[1] Duchesne, *Christian Worship*, p. 225.

IV. THE MOZARABIC RITE

*After the Priest has put on the sacred vestments, he says the
Responses.* Father, I have sinned against heaven, and before thee.[1]
Lord, have mercy. Our Father. Cleanse thou me from my secret
thoughts, *with the prayer* O God who makest the unworthy worthy.

Then he goes to the altar, and the Angelus having been said, he says:

In the name of our Lord Jesus Christ. Amen.
May the Grace of the Holy Ghost be with us.
I will go unto the altar of God.[2]
Give sentence with me, O God, &c. *with* Gloria.[2]

P.   I will go unto the altar of God;
R̸.   Even unto the God of my joy and gladness.[2]
P.   Vouchsafe, O Lord, this day;
R̸.   To keep us without sin.[3]
P.   O give thanks unto the Lord, for he is gracious:
R̸.   And his mercy endureth for ever.[4]
P.   Pray for us, O Holy Mother of God;
R̸.   That we may be made worthy of the promises of Christ.

I confess to God Almighty, to blessed Mary ever Virgin, to
blessed Michael the Archangel, to blessed John the Baptist, to
the holy Apostles Peter and Paul, to all the Saints, and to you,
brethren, that I have sinned exceedingly, in thought, word, and
deed, through my fault, through my fault, through my most
grievous fault. Therefore I pray blessed Mary ever Virgin,
blessed Michael the Archangel, blessed John the Baptist, the
holy Apostles Peter and Paul, all the Saints, and you, brethren,
to pray for me to the Lord our God.

The Ministers respond:

May Almighty God have mercy upon thee, and forgive thee
thy sins, and bring thee to everlasting life.
P. Amen.

[1] Luke 15[18].   [2] Ps. 43.
[3] Latin Version of *Te Deum*.   [4] Ps. 107[1].

Then the Ministers repeat the Confession.

P. May Almighty God have mercy upon you, forgive you your sins, and bring you to everlasting life. ℞. Amen.

P. May the Almighty and merciful God grant us pardon, absolution, and remission of our sins.

℞. Amen.

> *P.* Wilt thou not turn again, and quicken us;
> ℞. That thy people may rejoice in thee?[1]
> *P.* Shew us thy mercy, O Lord;
> ℞. And grant us thy salvation.[2]
> *P.* O Lord, hear my prayer;
> ℞. And let my cry come unto thee.
> *P.* The Lord be with you;
> ℞. And with thy spirit.

He says silently:

Take away from us we beseech thee, O Lord, all our iniquities and the spirit of pride and elation, which thou resistest; and fill us with the spirit of fear, and give us a humble and contrite heart, that despiseth not, that we may be worthy to enter the Holy of Holies with pure minds. Amen.

He at once goes up to the altar, and makes the sign of the cross over the altar, saying:

In the name of the Father, and of the Son, and of the Holy Ghost.

And having kissed the altar he recites the Antiphon of the cross: Hail precious cross *with four collects.*

Then with bowed head he says:

Through the glory of thy name, O Christ, Son of the living God, and through the intercession of S. Mary the virgin and blessed James and of all thy Saints, to aid and to have mercy on thine unworthy servants, and to be in the midst of us, O our God, who livest and reignest world without end. Amen.

[1] Ps. 85[6].   [2] Ps. 85[7].

Then he reads the Officium ad Missam [*i.e. the Introit*].

[*e.g. For the Epiphany.*

For as many of you as have been baptized into Christ have put on Christ; Alleluia.[1]

℣. Ye are the blessed of the Lord, who made heaven and earth.[2]

Or for Advent I.

Behold upon the mountains the feet of him that bringeth good tidings, Alleluia, that publisheth peace.[3] Alleluia, O Judah, keep thy solemn feasts, Alleluia, perform thy vows, Alleluia.[4]

℣. The Lord gave the word: great was the company of the preachers.[5]

Ps. And pay thy vows unto the most Highest. Alleluia.[6]

℣. Glory and honour be to the Father, and to the Son, and to the Holy Ghost, world without end. Amen.

Ps. And pay thy vows unto the most Highest. Alleluia. World without end. Amen.]

Except in Advent and Lent, Glory be to God on high *is said, in place of which on the Sunday before the feast of the Nativity of S. John the Baptist is said the Canticle* Benedictus.

World without end.

℟. Amen.

A Prayer, *before which* Let us pray *is not said, neither at the end* Through our Lord, *but only* Amen *is responded.*

[*e.g. Easter.*

To thee we ascribe praise, O Lord our God; and we beseech thy power that, as thou didst vouchsafe to die for us sinners, and didst again, after the third day, appear illustriously in the glory of resurrection; so we, absolved by thee, may merit to have in thee perpetual joy: in like manner as thou hast given us an example of true resurrection. ℟. Amen.

The Prayer finished, he goes to the middle of the altar, saying:

P. Through thy mercy, O our God, who art blessed, and livest and governest all things world without end.

℟. Amen.

---

[1] Gal. 3²⁷. [2] Ps. 115¹⁵. [3] Is. 52⁷. [4] Nah. 1¹⁵. [5] Ps. 68¹¹. [6] Ps. 50¹⁴.

Afterwards standing in the middle without turning to the people,
he says: The Lord be ever with you;
R̲. And with thy spirit.

The Lection of the Old Testament. (*e.g. The Book of the Pro-*
phet Isaiah.)

R̲. Thanks be to God.

At the end is said, Amen.
The Lord be ever with you;
R̲. And with thy spirit.

The Psalterium *or* Psallendo.

[*e.g. The Nativity.*

The Lord hath said unto me: Thou art my Son, this day have
I begotten thee.[1]

V̲. Desire of me, and I shall give thee the heathen for thine
inheritance: and the utmost parts of the earth for thy possession.[2]

Precentor. This day have I begotten thee.]

[*On the first five Sundays in Lent there follows a Missal Litany.*
On the first three they are addressed to our Lord, but on the last
two they are, more remarkably, put into his mouth. They are given
in Neale's Essays on Liturgiology, *pp.* 142 *ff.*]

Deacon: Keep silence.

The continuation of the Epistle of St. Paul to . . .

R̲. Thanks be to God.

At the end is said: Amen.

The Deacon asks a blessing.

The Lord be ever with you;
R̲. And with thy spirit.

The Lection of the Holy Gospel according to . . .

R̲. Glory be to thee, O Lord.

At the end is responded: Amen.

[1] Ps. 2⁷.   [2] Ps. 2⁸.

The Gospel being finished he says:

The Lord be ever with you;
℟. And with thy spirit.

Then is said Laus *or* Laudes.

[*e.g. The Nativity.*   Alleluia.

He sent redemption unto his people: he hath commanded his covenant for ever; holy and reverend is his Name. Alleluia.[1]]

While the Gospel is being sung the Lesser Missal *is brought, i.e. that in which the Proper of the Mass is contained, to the Epistle side.*

In the meanwhile when the Choir say the Alleluia, the Priest offers the Host with the Chalice and with the prayers which follow.

Acceptable to thy divine majesty, Almighty everlasting God, be the Oblation which we offer to thee for our sins and wickedness, and for the stability of the Holy Catholic Church and for those who hold the apostolic faith; through Christ our Lord. In the name of the Father, ✠ and of the Son, and of the Holy Ghost. Amen.

Putting down the Paten on the Corporal he then takes the Chalice, blessing it thus:

In the name of the Father, ✠ and of the Son, and of the Holy Ghost. Amen.

We offer unto thee, O Lord, the Chalice for blessing the Blood of Christ thy Son, and we beseech thy clemency, that it may ascend in the sight of thy divine Majesty with an odour of sweetness. Through the same Christ our Lord. Amen.

He places the Chalice on the altar, and takes the Chalice cover, without a blessing, and puts it on the Chalice, saying thus:

This Oblation we beseech thee, O Lord, be pleased to permit, and of all those offerers for whom it is offered, pardon from sin.[2] Through Christ our Lord. Amen.

---

[1] Ps. 111⁹.
[2] Et omnium offerentium eorum, pro quibus tibi offertur, peccata indulge.

And with joined hands inclining himself he says:

In the spirit of humility and with a contrite heart may we be accepted, O Lord, by thee, and may our sacrifice be so made to-day, that it may be pleasing unto thee, O Lord God.

Come, O Holy Ghost the Sanctifier, sanctify this sacrifice prepared for thee by my hands.

He puts incense in the thurible and censes the Sacrifice, if he pleases. Afterwards the Priest bows himself in the middle of the altar, with joined hands, and says in a loud voice:

Aid me, brethren, in your prayers, and pray to God for me.

R̲. May the Father, and the Son, and the Holy Ghost aid you.

Then the Choir say the Sacrificium, *and Antiphon similar to the Roman Offertory, and proper to each Office.*

[*e.g. The Nativity.*

For to us a child is born, unto us a son is given: and the government shall be upon his shoulder. Alleluia, Alleluia.[1]]

The Priest takes the water in his hands and says silently, with three fingers over the Oblation:

In the name of the Father, ✠ and of the Son, and of the Holy Ghost. Amen.

He bows himself before the altar and says in silence that prayer.

I will draw near to thee in the humility of my spirit, that I may speak to thee, because of the great hope and strength that thou hast given to me. Thou therefore, O Son of David, when the Mystery was revealed thou camest to us in the flesh, open thou the secrets of my heart with the key of thy cross, sending one of the Seraphin, with that burning coal, which was taken from thine altar, that it may cleanse my soiled lips, enlighten my mind, may furnish teaching matter; that my tongue which serves to the profit of my neighbours through love, may sound the end of error, but may resound of the truth through thee, without end of preaching, O my God, who livest and reignest world without end. Amen.

[1] Is. 9⁶.

Thus far is the Mass of the Catechumens. He begins the Mass Proper, saying thus:

The Lord be ever with you;
℟. And with thy spirit.

He says the Oratio Missae, *i.e. collect of the day, which varies with the Mass. Amen is responded.*

The Priest says:

Through thy mercy, O our God, who art blessed, and livest and governest all things world without end.
℟. Amen.

The Priest says, elevating his hanas:

Let us pray.

The Choir respond:

Agios, Agios, Agios Lord God, King eternal, praise and thanks be to thee.

Afterwards the Priest says:

Let us have in mind in our prayers the Holy Catholic Church, that the merciful Lord may vouchsafe to increase it in faith and hope and love. Let us have in mind all them that are lapsed, that are captive, that are sick, that are strangers; that the merciful Lord would vouchsafe to redeem, strengthen, and to comfort them.

The Choir respond: Grant it, Almighty eternal God.

The Priest says another prayer, agreeing with the Office (usually called Alia Oratio).

[*e.g. Epiphany IV.*

We bear, O Lord, the yoke of our iniquities with a hard neck, a downcast countenance, a contrite heart. And scarcely have we learned by our punishment to repent, who before it would not recognize our guilt. But thou, O Lord, who hast made tame wild beasts in the den, and hast made cool the flames in the heat of the furnace, lift up thy hand to help us, and grant us the most safe support of thy defence in affliction. That us, whom the weight of sins bows down, the virtue of thy long-suffering may lift up; and that, since by our iniquities we have fallen to the ground, we may be mercifully raised by thine ineffable goodness, that us whom the actions of divers transgressions convict, the indulgence of thy mercy may acquit. R̲. Amen.]

The Priest says:

Through thy mercy, O our God, in whose sight the names of the holy Apostles and Martyrs, Confessors and Virgins, are recited. R̲. Amen.

The Priest says:

Our Priests offer the Oblation to the Lord God: the Pope of Rome and the rest for themselves and for all the Clergy and people of the Church committed to them, and for all the brotherhood; also all the priests, deacons, clerks, and all the people standing around offer it in honour of the Saints, for themselves and theirs.

Choir:

They offer it for themselves and for all the brotherhood.

The Priest says:

Commemorating the most blessed Apostles and Martyrs, the glorious Holy Mary the Virgin, Zacharias, John, the Innocents, Peter, Paul, John, James, Andrew, Philip, Thomas, Bartholomew, Matthew, James, Simon and Jude, Matthias, Mark, and Luke.

Choir:

And of all the Martyrs.

The Priest says:

Also for the spirits of them that are at rest, Hilary, Athanasius, Martin, Ambrose, Augustine, Fulgentius, Leander, Isidore, David, Julian, &c.[1]

The Choir respond:

And of all that are at rest.

[1] Thirty-five other Saints are named here; among them are Martin and Roderick.

The Collect after the Names *is recited, agreeing with the Office of the day.*

[*e.g. Advent V.*

We beseech thee, Lord Jesus, our God, that we, who faithfully wait for thine Advent, may not incur everlasting punishment; by which thine Advent grant pardon to them that offer, and rest eternal to them that are departed.

℞. Amen.]

The Priest says:

Because thou art the life of the living, the health of the sick, and the rest of all the faithful departed in eternity, world without end. ℞. Amen.

The Prayer for Peace *is said by the Priest, agreeing with the Office of the day.*

[*e.g. Lent I.*

Saviour of the world, Word of the eternal Father, who, after receiving the faith of the woman, didst abide with the Samaritans two days at their request; that under the type of those two days might mystically be commended the number of the two precepts, that is, love to God, and love to our neighbour: &c., &c.

℞. Amen.]

These things being finished the Priest says:

For thou art our true peace and unbroken love, who livest and reignest with thee and the Holy Ghost, One God, world without end. Amen.

The Priest says, lifting up his hands toward heaven:

The Grace of God the Father Almighty, the peace and love of our Lord Jesus Christ, and the communion of the Holy Ghost, be ever with us all.

℞. And with all of good-will.

The Priest says:

As ye stand, give the peace.

℞. Peace I leave with you, my peace I give unto you: not

as the world giveth, give I unto you.[1] A new commandment
I give unto you, that ye love one another.[2]

℞. My peace I give unto you.

℣. Glory and honour be to the Father, and to the Son, and to
the Holy Ghost world without end.

℞. My peace.

In the meanwhile when the Choir say My peace *the Priest takes
the Pax, saying thus:*

Receive the Kiss of Peace and love that ye may be fit for the
sacred Mysteries of God.

*And immediately he gives the Peace to the Deacon or boy, and the
boy to the people.*

And then the Priest bows down and with joined hands says:

I will go unto the altar of God.

℞. Even unto the God of my joy and gladness.[3]

The Priest puts his hand over the Chalice and says:

> Your ears to the Lord;
> ℞. We have them to the Lord.[4]
> P. Lift up your hearts;
> ℞. We lift them up unto the Lord.[5]

The priest says, inclining himself and with joined hands:

Unto God, and our Lord Jesus Christ the Son of God, who is
in heaven, let us render worthy praises and worthy thanks.

℞. It is meet and just.

The Illation *follows, different for each Sunday and festival.* [*In
all* 156 *are found in this rite.*]

[*e.g. The Nativity.*

It is meet and just, most merciful Father, that we should
render to thine omnipotence and loving-kindness that which thou
hast enabled us to bestow. Because on this day, after long time,

---

[1] John 14[27].   [2] John 13[34].   [3] Ps. 43.
[4] *Habemus ad Dominum.*   [5] *Levamus ad Dominum*
This is the only Liturgy (Western) that uses the word *Levamus* here.

but no long time ago, he who belonged always to thee and to himself, Christ Jesus, thine only-begotten Son, is born to us. He was made the Son of his handmaiden, the Lord of his mother. The birth of Mary; the fruit of the Church. By the one he is produced; by the other he is received. He that as an infant comes forth from the one, is set forth as the Wonderful by the other. The one produced salvation for the peoples; the other the peoples themselves. The one bore the life in her womb; the other in her laver. In the limbs of the one Christ is infused; by the waters of the other Christ is endued. By the one he that was is born; by the other he that had perished is found. In the one the Redeemer of the nations is quickened; in the other the nations are vivified. By the one he came, that he might take away sins; by the other he took away the sins for the which he came. By the one he deplored us; by the other he cured us, &c. *It develops thus:* Wherefore now, standing at his right hand in happy and glorious perennity, she, with all angels, praises and lauds him that reigneth with thee, Almighty Father, and with the Holy Ghost, saying:]

Holy, Holy, Holy, O Lord God of Sabaoth.
Heaven and earth are full of thy glorious Majesty.
Hosanna to the son of David. Hosanna in the highest.

Blessed is he that cometh in the name of the Lord.
Hosanna in the highest.
Agios, Agios, Agios, O Lord God.

THE CANON *begins*[1]

The Post-Sanctus. *The Priest recites a short prayer according to the Office of the day.*

[*e.g. The Nativity.*

Truly holy, truly blessed is our Lord Jesus Christ, thy Son, who came from heaven, that he might dwell upon earth: was made flesh that he might dwell in us, Christ the Lord and everlasting redeemer.]

[1] I am indebted to Dr. L. Pullan for permission to use the translation of the text of the Mozarabic Canon given in his *History of the Book of Common Prayer*, pp. 314, 315, Longmans, 1929.

Then the Priest says in silence with joined hands, bowing himself before the altar, this prayer:

Be present, be present, Jesu the good High Priest, in the midst of us as thou wast in the midst of thy disciples and hal✠low this oblation that we may take the things ✠ sanctified by the hands of thy holy angel, Holy Lord, and everlasting Redeemer.

Immediately follows the formula of Consecration . . .

Our Lord Jesus Christ on the night in which he was betrayed, took bread, and giving thanks, he bles✠sed and brake it: and gave it to his disciples saying, Take, and eat.

This is My Body which shall be given for you.

Here the Body is elevated.

As often as ye shall eat it, do this in remembrance ✠ of Me.

Likewise also the cup after he supped, saying,

This ✠ is the cup of the New Testament in My Blood, which shall be shed for you and for many for the remission of sins.

Here the Chalice is elevated covered with the 'Filiola'.

As often as ye shall drink it, do this in remembrance ✠ of Me.

R̷. Amen.

As often as ye shall eat this bread and drink this cup, ye shall shew forth the Lord's death, until he come in brightness ✠ from heaven.

The Post-Pridie Prayer *is said, differing in different Masses.*

[*e.g. The Nativity.*

Keeping, O Lord, these thy gifts and commandments, we set forth upon thine altar the burnt offerings of bread and wine, beseeching the most abundant goodness of thy mercy, that by the same spirit, by whom undefiled virginity conceived thee in the flesh, the undivided Trinity may hallow these offerings, &c.]

Afterwards the Priest says:

Thou granting it, holy Lord, because thou for us thine unworthy servants dost create all these right good things, dost hallow, ✠ quicken, ✠ bless, ✠ and bestow them upon us; that they may be blessed by thee our God for ever and ever.

R̷. Amen.

He takes the Body of the Lord from the Paten and puts it over the uncovered Chalice and says:

> The Lord be ever with you;
> ℞. And with thy spirit.

The Priest says:

The faith which we believe with the heart, let us say with the mouth.

He elevates the Body of Christ, in order that it may be seen by all the people.
And all together say the Symbolum, i.e.
The Creed.[1]
We believe in one God, &c.

In the meanwhile the Priest breaks the Host through the middle into two parts, and taking one part he makes from it five particles and places them on the Paten in a straight line, and each one has a proper name. Taking likewise the other part he makes from it four particles and arranges them on the Paten, in the order thus expressed:

	The Incarnation.	
The Death.	The Nativity.	The Resurrection.
	The Circumcision.	
	The Apparition.	The Glory.
	The Passion.	The Kingdom.

He at once thoroughly cleanses his fingers, and covers the Chalice, he prays silently for the Faithful living, or makes Remembrance for the living. Now all these things are to be completed while the Choir sing the Creed.

[1] Evidently two by two, 'bini ac bini'.

Then he recites the Lord's Prayer, prefacing it with a short Preface, which varies with each Mass.

[*e.g. The Nativity.*

He shows us that Way that we might follow, that Life he taught so that we might speak out, that Truth he instructed that we might hold fast unto thee, great Father, with trembling hearts we proclaim from earth:

Our Father, which art in heaven.	R̴. Amen.
Hallowed be thy Name.	R̴. Amen.
Thy kingdom come.	R̴. Amen.
Thy will be done on earth as it is in heaven.	R̴. Amen.
Give us this day our daily bread.	R̴. For thou art God.
And forgive us our trespasses as we forgive them that trespass against us.	R̴. Amen.

And lead us not into temptation.
R̴. But deliver us from evil.

The Priest says:

Delivered from evil, confirmed always in good, may we be found worthy to serve thee, our God and Lord. (*He strikes his breast.*) Put an end to our sins, O Lord: give joy to the sorrowful, give redemption to the captives, health to the sick, rest to the departed; Grant peace and security in all our days. Destroy the boldness of our enemies, and graciously hear, O God, the prayers of all thy faithful Christian servants this day and at all time. Through thy Son Jesus Christ our Lord, who with thee liveth and reigneth in the Unity of the Holy Spirit God, world without end. R̴. Amen.

Thus the Priest should do: He takes the Particle, which is called the Glory, *from the Paten and puts it over the Chalice. In Eastertide evidently he may say three times alternately:*

The lion of the tribe of Judah, the Root of David, hath prevailed, Alleluia.[1] *And each time the Choir may respond 'qualibet vice'.*

Thou that sittest upon the Cherubin, Root of David, Alleluia.

[1] Rev. 5⁵.

After that he may say this prayer, to himself, in a low voice:

Holy things to Holy Persons, and may the commixture of the Body (and Blood) of our Lord Jesus Christ, be to us that receive it and drink it for pardon; and be vouchsafed to the departed faithful for rest. Amen.

And he places the Particle into the Chalice and says in a loud voice thus, if there be no Deacon present:

> Bow down yourselves for the blessing.
> The Lord be ever with you.
> R̠. And with thy spirit.

Then the Benediction in three distinct clauses is bestowed, Amen is responded to each one. The Blessing varies with the Office of the day.

[*e.g. The Nativity.*

O Lord Jesus Christ, who once on this day didst vouchsafe to be born for us: that he himself might quicken you by his own nativity.
R̠. Amen.

And who, taking childhood, was clothed with the garments of low humanity, might clothe us with the vesture of heavenly powers.
R̠. Amen.

And may it be the food of your inmost hearts, which placed in the manger to appear to those that believe, he willed himself to be fed upon.
R̠. Amen.

Through the mercy of our God himself, who is blessed and liveth and governeth all things world without end.
R̠. Amen.

> The Lord be ever with you.
> R̠. And with thy spirit.

The Choir say:

O Taste, and see, how gracious the Lord is,[1] Alleluia. Alleluia. Alleluia. I will alway give thanks unto the Lord: his praise shall ever be in my mouth. Alleluia. Alleluia. Alleluia.[2]

The Lord delivereth the souls of his servants: and all they that put their trust in him shall not be destitute.[3] Alleluia. Alleluia.

---

[1] Ps. 34[8].   [2] Ps. 34[1].   [3] Ps. 34[22].

Alleluia. Glory and honour be to the Father, and to the Son, and to the Holy Ghost, world without end.

While the Choir are singing O Taste, *and see the Priest takes the Particle following, which is called the* Glory, *and places it over the Chalice and says silently this prayer:*

I will take the bread of heaven from the Lord's Table and will call upon the name of the Lord.

And the Priest says the Remembrance for the Dead, *holding that Particle over the Chalice, and having said the* Remembrance *he says these prayers, which follow:*

O Lord my God, grant me so to receive the Body and Blood of thy Son our Lord Jesus Christ, that I may deserve through them to obtain remission of all my sins, and to be filled with thy Holy Ghost. Who livest and reignest world without end. Amen.

Hail evermore, most holy Flesh of Christ, the sum of delight unto eternity; I will take the bread of heaven and will call upon the name of the Lord.

He makes the sign of the cross with the Host and consumes the Particle, which he holds in his hand, and covers the Chalice and comes to the Paten and consumes all the Particles in order, first taking those which were put last on the Paten. And at once he gives the Communion to the people. And then he takes the Paten and puts it over the Chalice, and thoroughly cleanses it with his finger and thumb and says this prayer:

Hail evermore, heavenly drink, which to me above all things and over all things art sweet.

May the Body and Blood of our Lord Jesus Christ preserve my body and soul unto eternal life. Amen.

He receives the Blood, and while the Priest consumes the Blood, he says at once this prayer:

O Lord my God, Father, and Son, and Holy Ghost; make me ever to seek thee and to love thee, and through this Holy Communion which I have taken, never to depart from thee, for thou art God and there is none beside thee world without end. Amen.

The Choir sing the Communion:

Refreshed by the Body and Blood of Christ we praise thee, O Lord, Alleluia. Alleluia. Alleluia.

When he has finished the ablutions, he carries down the Lesser Missal, and it is put on the Epistle side, the Book from which the Mass is recited from the beginning to the end. Then the Priest says at the side of the altar, this prayer:

Refreshed by the Body and Blood of Christ, and likewise sanctified, Let us return thanks unto God the Father Almighty, that we having the same resurrection and sanctification here, and in the future, may we obtain glory everlasting.

R̂. Amen.

The Priest says in the middle of the altar:

Through thy mercy, O our God, who art blessed and livest and governest all things world without end. R̂. Amen.

　　　　P. The Lord be ever with you;
　　　　R̂. And with thy spirit.

He says in the middle of the altar:

The solemnities are completed in the name of our Lord Jesus Christ; let our vow be accepted with peace.

R̂. Thanks be to God.

[*Or in Ferial Masses:*

It is Dismissal in the name of our Lord Jesus Christ, let us complete it with peace.

R̂. Thanks be to God.]

Lastly with bent knees before the altar, he recites Hail, Holy Queen *with the prayer* Grant us thy servants, we beseech thee, O Lord God, to enjoy perpetual health of mind and body; and by the glorious intercession of blessed Mary ever Virgin, to be delivered from present sorrow and to enjoy everlasting gladness. Through our Lord . . .

And turning toward the people he gives them a blessing, saying:

In Unity of the Holy Ghost, the Father and Son bless you. Amen.

And immediately he comes down from the altar. And be it noted that the Priest never turns himself toward the people, unless when he bestows this last blessing, and when he says: Aid me, brethren, in your prayers.

(Francis Ximenes added to the Gothic Office the Confession after the Roman custom and other prayers before the Introit, and the Antiphon, Hail, Holy Queen, *at the end.)*

(The order of the Office is very different in Masses of the Dead. The Confession having been recited, the Priest says in the middle of the altar: Lift up yourselves. The Lord be ever with you. *And immediately he commences the Introit:* Thou art my hope and my portion, Alleluia, in the land of the living, Alleluia.[1] *The* Alleluia *is omitted during Lent. That we might omit others, he prays at the breaking of the Host:* Rest eternal may the Lord give unto thee, May light perpetual shine upon thee, and may thy soul be filled with brightness, and thy bones be made alive again from their place.)

[1] Ps. 142[6].

V. THE STOWE MISSAL

ORDINARY OF THE MASS

The Litany of the Holy Apostles and Martyrs and of the Virgins begins.

O God, make speed to save us.[1]

We have sinned, O Lord, we have sinned, spare our sins, and save us; thou who guidedst Noah over the flood waves, hear us; who with thy word recalledst Jonah from the abyss; deliver us; who stretchedst forth thy hand to Peter as he sank, help us, O Christ.

Son of God, thou didst the marvellous things of the Lord with our fathers, be favourable in our days also; Stretch forth thy hand from on high.

Deliver us, O Christ.
Hear us, O Christ.

Saint Mary	Kyrie eleison.
" Peter	Saint Madianus.
" Paul	" Mark.
" Andrew	" Luke.
" James	All the saints pray for us.
" Bartholomew	Be favourable, spare us, O Lord;
" Thomas	Be favourable, deliver us, O Lord;
" Matthew	From all evil deliver us, O Lord;
" James	By thy Cross deliver us, O Lord.

A PRAYER OF S. AUGUSTINE[2]

All our righteousnesses are unclean (profeta?[3]) as a filthy rag; we are not worthy, O Lord Christ, that we should live; but thou, God, willest not the death of a sinner; grant pardon unto us that are made of flesh, that through penitential labours we may enjoy eternal life in heaven. Through our Lord.

[1] The second Versicle at Matins.

[2] These words are the ending of the prayer of S. Ambrose; see Warren, *L.R.C.C.*, p. 249, note 6.

[3] This may mean 'as says the Prophet'. See Is. 64[6] (A.V.).

I implore thee, most high God of Sabaoth, Holy Father, that thou wouldest deign to gird me with the tunic of love, and to encompass my loins with the belt of thy love, and to burn up the reins of my heart with the fire of thy love, so that I may be able to intercede for my sins and to earn pardon for the sins of the people here present, and to sacrifice a peace offering for each one; Me also, when with boldness I fall before thee, let not thou perish, but vouchsafe to wash, to adorn, and to raise up gently; Through our Lord.

This prayer is sung in every Mass:

Let our prayer ascend to the throne of thy glory, O Lord, and let not our supplication return to us unprofitable; through . . .

In the Solemnities of Peter and Christ:[1]

O God, who by giving the keys of the kingdom of heaven didst confer upon thy blessed Apostle Peter the Pontifical power of binding and loosing souls, favourably receive our prayers, and by his intercession, Lord, we ask help, that we may be loosed from the chains of our sins. Through our Lord.

THE ANGELIC HYMN

Glory be to God on high, and on earth peace to men of good will. We praise thee, we bless thee, we adore thee, we glorify thee, we magnify thee, we give thanks to thee for thy great mercy, O Lord, heavenly king, God the Father Almighty; O Lord the only-begotten Son of God, Jesu Christ, Holy Spirit of God, and we all say Amen; O Lord, Son of God the Father, Lamb of God that takest away the sins of the world, have mercy upon us, receive our prayers, thou that sittest at the right hand of God the Father, have mercy upon us; for thou only art holy, thou only art the Lord, thou only art glorious with the Holy Spirit in the glory of God the Father. Amen.

This prayer is said on behalf of those who transgress daily:

O God who art offended by transgression, and art appeased by penitence, behold the groaning of the afflicted, and mercifully turn away those evils which thou justly inflictest. Through, &c.

[1] Probably a clerical error for Paul.

Prayers and supplications of compassion of the Roman Church. This prayer first of Peter.

O God, who hast prepared for them that love thee such good things as cannot be seen, pour into our hearts the inclination to love thee, that we loving thee in all things and above all things may obtain thy promises, which exceed all that we can desire. Through our Lord.

Here is amplification.[1]

The Lection of the Apostle Paul to the Corinthians begins.

1 Cor. 11[20-2]

Brethren, when therefore ye assemble . . . condemned with the world.

O God, who by ruling preservest us, by sparing justifiest us, deliver us from temporal tribulation, and bestow upon us eternal joys. Through our Lord, &c.

Almighty and everlasting God, who hast redeemed thy people by the Blood of thine only-begotten One, break up the works of Satan, burst the chains of sin, so that they who by the confession of thy holy name have obtained eternal life, may owe nothing to the author of death. Through, &c.

Seek the Lord and his strength; seek his face evermore.[2]

Give thanks unto the Lord, call upon his name, make known his deeds among the people. Sing unto him, sing psalms unto him, talk ye of all his wondrous works. Glory ye in his holy name: let the heart of them rejoice that seek the Lord.[3]

May the gifts be acceptable (grata) unto thee, O Lord, with which the mysteries of our liberty and life are celebrated. Through, &c. Alleluia.

The Lord is my strength and my song: and is become my salvation.[4]

Look, we beseech thee, O Lord, with favour upon these offerings, that it may serve our devotion (devotioni) to salvation.

---

[1] See Introduction, p. 10.
[2] Ps. 105[4].
[3] 1 Chron. 16[8-10] (A.V.).
[4] Ps. 118[14].

The prayer of S. Martin for the people begins.

Amen. Thanks be to God.

1. Let us all say: 'O Lord, hear us and have mercy upon us, Lord have mercy', with our whole heart and mind.

2. Who looketh upon the earth and maketh it to tremble.

R̷. We pray (to thee, O Lord, to hear and to have mercy).[1]

3. For profound peace and tranquillity from above, in our time, for the Holy Catholic Church which is from one end of the earth to the other.

R̷. We pray, &c.

4. For our Pastor, the Bishop, and for all bishops, and priests, and deacons, and all clergy.

R̷. We pray, &c.

5. For this place, and for those who dwell therein, for our most devout Emperor and all the Roman Army.

R̷. We pray, &c.

6. For all who have been set in high places, for virgins, widows, and orphans.

R̷. We pray, &c.

7. For those sojourning abroad, and travelling by the road, and sailing and penitents, and Catechumens.

R̷. We pray, &c.

8. Let us be mindful of the holy Apostles and Martyrs, that by their prayers for us, we may gain pardon.

R̷. We pray, &c.

9. Let us pray for a Christian and peaceful end to be granted us by the Lord. Grant it, O Lord, grant it.

10. And let us entreat the holy Lord for the divine bond of love to continue in us.

R̷. Grant it.

---

[1] The portion in brackets is not in the text; but see Duchesne, *Christian Worship*, p. 9.

11. Let us entreat the Lord to preserve the sanctity and purity of the Catholic faith.

R̴. Grant it.

Let us say, &c.

Favourably regard, O Lord, the sacrifice which is to be offered unto thee; that it may both cleanse us from the corruptions of our present state, and make us acceptable unto thy name, through our Lord.

I stand before the witness of thine eyes, O Lord, accused by my conscience: I dare not ask for others what I am not worthy to obtain; for thou knowest, O Lord, all things which are done within us; we blush to confess that sin of whose committing we are not afraid; by words only do we yield ourselves to thee, we deceive with the heart, and by our deeds we prove what we say we intend (quod velle nos dicimus nostris actibus adprobamus). Spare us, O Lord, when we confess, forgive us when we sin, have mercy upon us when we pray to thee; but because in thy Sacraments my understanding is weak, vouchsafe, O Lord, who receivest not with a hard heart the words which we speak, of thyself to bestow forgiveness upon us, through our Lord.

A half-uncovering here.

Let my prayer be set forth in thy sight as the incense: and let the lifting up of my hands be as an evening sacrifice.[1]

It is sung three times. The linen cloth is lifted up from the Chalice.

Come, O Lord, the Almighty Sanctifier, and bless this sacrifice prepared for thee.

It is sung three times.

The reading of the Gospel according to S. John begins.
John 6[51-7]

Our Lord Jesus Christ said, I am the living bread . . . shall live by me.

[*In the manuscript there is a mutilated leaf here two-thirds of which is cut away. On the right side are written the words from the Prayer of Gregory, and the rest. The left side is blank.*]

[1] Ps. 141[2].

The Prayer of Gregory over the Gospel.

We beseech thee, O Lord, Almighty God, that thou wouldest mercifully regard our prayers offered to thee, and extend the right hand of thy Majesty to our defence, through our Lord.

I believe in One God, &c. [*The 'Filioque' clause is omitted.*]

A full uncovering here.

Shew us thy mercy, O Lord: and grant us thy salvation.[1]

It is sung three times.

Sanctify, O Lord, the gifts offered to thee, and cleanse us from the stains of our sins. Through our Lord.

We beseech thee, O Lord, to receive with favour the offerings of our devotion, and through the glorious sacrifice of thy servants purify our hearts. Through our Lord.

We offer unto thee, O Lord Jesus Christ, these oblations and pure drink-offerings,[2] who suffered for us and rose again the third day from the dead, for the souls of our beloved brethren N. and sisters N. whose names we recite, and whosever names we do not recite but are recited by thee in the book of life eternal; for thy mercy save them, who reignest world without end. Amen.

The second part is here added over the Offerings.

May this Oblation of thy people be pleasing unto thee, which we offer to thee in honour of our Lord Jesus Christ, and in commemoration of thy blessed Apostles, and thy Martyrs, and confessors, whose relics here we specially call to mind N.,[3] and of those whose festival is celebrated to-day; and for the souls of all our bishops, and our priests and our deacons, and our beloved brethren and our beloved sisters, and our boys and our girls, and penitents; may [our Oblations] avail for them all to salvation, through our Lord.

> Lift up your hearts.
> We lift them up unto the Lord.
> Let us give thanks unto our Lord God.
> It is meet and right.

[1] Ps. 85⁷.   [2] sincera labamina.
[3] quorum hic reliquias spicialiter recolimus.

It is truly meet and right, just and for our salvation, that we should here at all times and in all places give thanks unto thee, Holy Lord, Almighty everlasting God, through Christ our Lord, who together with thine Only-begotten and the Holy Ghost art one and immortal God, incorruptible and immovable God, invisible and faithful God, wonderful and praiseworthy God, honourable and strong God, most high and magnificent God, living and true God, wise and powerful God, holy and beautiful God, great and good God, terrible and peace-loving God, noble and upright God, pure and kind God, blessed and just God, righteous and holy God, not in the singleness of one person, but in the Trinity of one substance. We believe in thee, we bless thee, we worship thee, and we praise thy name ever world without end; through whom is the salvation of the world, through whom is the life of men, through whom is the resurrection of the dead.

Here the 'dignum' receives the addition if 'per quem' follows in the text.[1]

Through whom the angels praise thy majesty, the Dominions adore, the Powers tremble, the heavens and the heavenly hosts together with the blessed Seraphin in triumphant chorus unite to celebrate thy Majesty; with these we entreat thee to bid our voices also be admitted, saying with lowly praise: Holy.

Here the 'dignum' receives the addition if 'sanctus' is in the text.[1]

Holy, Holy, Holy, Lord God of Sabaoth; the heavens and the whole earth are full of thy glory. Osanna in the highest, blessed is he that cometh in the Name of the Lord; Osanna in the highest, blessed is he that came from heaven that he might dwell on earth, was made man that he might destroy the sins of the flesh, was made a victim that through his passion he might give eternal life to them that believe. Through our Lord.

CANON OF POPE GELASIUS

Thee therefore, O most Merciful Father, through Jesus Christ, thy Son our Lord, we humbly pray and entreat that thou wouldest accept and bless these gifts, these offerings, this holy and

[1] Probably refers to the Proper Preface on Festivals.

unspotted Sacrifice, which we offer unto thee in the first place for thy Holy Catholic Church that thou wouldest be pleased to keep it in peace, to preserve, unite, and govern it throughout the world; and also for thy most blessed servant N., our Pope, bishop of the Apostle's throne, and all the orthodox, worshipping in the Apostolic faith, and our Abbot Bishop N.

Here are recited the names of the living.

Remember also, O Lord, thy servants N., thy handmaidens N., and all here present, whose faith and devotion are known to Thee, for whom we offer unto Thee, this sacrifice of praise for themselves, and all pertaining to them, for the redemption of their souls, for the good estate of their heads of houses (Pro stratu seniorum)[1] and for the purity of all ministers, for the chastity of virgins, the continence of widows, for seasonable weather, and for the fruitfulness of the fruits of the earth, for the return of peace, and the end of dangers, for the safety of kings, and the peace of peoples, and the return of captives, for the prayers of those present, for the memory of the Martyrs, for the remission of our sins, and the correction of their deeds, and the repose of the dead, and the prosperity of our journey, for the Lord Bishop the Pope, and all bishops and priests, and every order in the Church, for the Roman empire and all Christian kings, for our brothers and sisters, for the brethren 'in the straight way', for the brethren whom from the thick darkness of this world the Lord has vouchsafed to summon, that the divine goodness may receive them in eternal peace of great light, for the brethren who are afflicted with various kinds of sorrows, that the divine goodness may vouchsafe to care for them, for the hope of their safety and salvation, who pay their vows to thee the eternal, living, and true God. Joining in Communion with . . . [*In the Stowe Missal there are seven clauses inserted here for different festivals; we give those for the Nativity, the Circumcision, and Easter.*]

The Nativity.

And celebrating this most Holy day, in which a spotless Virgin brought forth a Saviour into this world.

[1] See Warren, *L.R.C.C.*, p. 260, note 61.

The Circumcision.

And celebrating this most Holy day of the Circumcision of our Lord Jesus Christ.

Easter.

And celebrating this most Holy day (*or* night) of the resurrection of our Lord Jesus Christ.]

... and reverently commemorating first the glorious and ever Virgin Mary, Mother of our God and Lord Jesus Christ; as also thy blessed Apostles and Martyrs Peter, Paul, Andrew, James, John, Thomas, James, Philip, Bartholomew, Matthew, Simon and Thaddaeus, Linus, Cletus, Clement, Xystus, Cornelius, Cyprian, Lawrence, Chrysogonus, John and Paul, Cosmas and Damian, and of all thy Saints, through whose merits and prayers do thou grant that in all things we may be defended by the help of thy protection. Through Christ our Lord.

This Oblation therefore of the service of us and of thy whole family, which we offer unto Thee in honour of our Lord Jesus Christ, and in commemoration of thy blessed Martyrs, in this church which thy servants built to the honour of thy glorious name; we beseech thee, O Lord, graciously to accept and that thou wouldest deliver him[1] and all people from idol worship, and turn them to thee the true God and Father Almighty. Through our Lord.

Which Oblation do thou Almighty God, we beseech thee, vouchsafe in all respects to make blessed, ✠ approved, and ratified, reasonable, and acceptable, that it may become unto us the Body and Blood of thy most dearly beloved Son, Jesus Christ our Lord.

Who the day before he suffered, took bread into his holy and venerable hands, and with eyes lifted up to heaven, to thee, O God, his Father Almighty, he gave thanks to thee, he blessed, brake, gave to His disciples, saying: Take, and eat ye all of this, For this is my Body.

Likewise after supper, he took also the Cup into his holy and venerable hands, also giving thanks unto thee, he blessed, gave,

[1] Refers to a particular church, the founder being still alive. See Warren, *L.R.C.C.*, p. 259, note 57.

to his disciples, saying: Take, and drink ye all of this, for this is the Cup of my holy Blood of the New and eternal Testament, the Mystery of faith, which for you and for many shall be shed for remission of sins. As often as ye shall do these things, ye shall do them in remembrance of me. Ye shall shew forth my passion, ye shall proclaim my resurrection, ye shall hope for my coming, till I come again to you from heaven.[1]

Wherefore, O Lord, we thy servants and likewise thy holy people, are mindful of the blessed passion of thy Son Christ our Lord, his resurrection from the dead, and his glorious ascension into heaven: offer unto thy most excellent Majesty of thine own gifts and bounties, a spotless Host, a holy Host, a pure Host, the holy bread of eternal life and the Cup of everlasting salvation.

Upon which things vouchsafe to look with a propitious and serene countenance, and accept them as thou didst vouchsafe to accept the presents of thy just servant Abel and the sacrifice of our patriarch Abraham, and that which thy high priest Melchisedech offered to thee, a holy sacrifice, a spotless Host.

We humbly beg, and entreat thee, Almighty God, command these things to be carried by the hands of thy holy Angel to thine Altar on high in the sight of thy divine Majesty that as many of us as shall by the participation of the Altar of holiness receive the most holy Body and Blood of thy Son, may be filled with all benediction and grace.

Remember also, O Lord, the names of those who have gone before us with the sign of faith and rest in the sleep of peace, together with all holy and venerable priests who in the whole world offer the spiritual sacrifice to God the Father, and Son, and Holy Ghost, the priest N., head of our house,[2] offers sacrifice for himself and all pertaining to him, and for the company of the whole Catholic Church; and for commemorating the order of those at rest the venerable patriarchs, prophets, Apostles, and Martyrs, and all Saints also, that they may deign to prevail upon the Lord our God for us.

[1] Cp. Ambrosian Canon.   [2] See note, p. 79.

G

[*In the Stowe Missal there follows a Litany of Saints. There are thirty-one names in all. We give a selection and the ending of the Litany.*]

Saint Stephen	pray for us.
Saint Martin	pray for us.
Saint Jerome	pray for us.
Saint Augustine	pray for us.
Saint Columba	pray for us.
Saint Comgallus	pray for us.
Saint Cannicha	pray for us.
Saint Kevin	pray for us.
Saint Ite [or Ythe]	pray for us.

Be favourable. Spare us, O Lord. Be favourable.
Deliver us, O Lord, from all evil.
Deliver us, O Lord, by thy Cross.
Deliver us, O Lord, sinners.
We beseech thee, to hear us.
Son of God, We beseech thee to hear us.
We ask thee that thou wouldest give peace.
O Lamb of God, hear us.
Who takest away the sins of the world, have mercy upon us.
O Christ, hear us. O Christ, hear us. O Christ, hear us.

THE PRAYER OF AMBROSE

I stand, O God, before the sight of thy divine Majesty, who presume to call upon thy holy Name; have mercy upon me, O Lord, a man, a sinner, sunk in the mire and refuse of uncleanness; pardon, O Lord, thy unworthy priest by whose hands this Oblation seems to be offered; spare, O Lord, a sinner polluted with the taint above all of mortal sins, and enter not into judgement with thy servant, O Lord, for in thy sight shall no man living be justified:[1] we indeed are weighed down by the weaknesses and desires of the flesh: remember, O Lord, that we are flesh, and that there is none other to be compared to thee; in thy sight even the heavens are not clean, how much more we that are men, earthy and unclean like a filthy rag. We are not worthy, Jesu Christ,

[1] Ps. 143[2].

that we should live, but thou who willest not the death of a sinner, grant unto us who are set in the flesh pardon, that through the labours of penitence we may enjoy eternal life in the heavens.[1]

[*Here again follows another long list of names, including the following:*]

Abel, Enoch, Noah, Isaac, David, Daniel, Esther, Tobias, Luke, Cyprian, Colman, Sildas, Laurence, Melletus, Justus, &c.,[2] and all at rest, who have gone before us in the peace of the Lord, from Adam to the present day, whose name God hath named and knoweth; to them and to all that rest in Christ, grant, we beseech thee, a place of refreshment, light, and peace.

To us also thy sinful servants, trusting in the multitude of thy mercies, vouchsafe to grant some part and fellowship with thy holy Apostles and Martyrs, with Peter, Paul, Patrick, John, Stephen, Matthias, Barnabas, Ignatius, Alexander, Marcellinus, Peter, Perpetua, Agnes, Cecilia, Felicitas, Anastasia, Agatha, Lucy, and with all thy Saints, into whose company we beseech thee to admit us, not weighing our merits but pardoning our offences. Through, &c.

By whom, O Lord, thou dost ever create, hallow, quicken, bless and bestow upon us all these good things.

By him, and with him, and in him, be unto thee, O God the Father Almighty, in the Unity of the Holy Ghost, all honour and glory, world without end.

It is sung three times. Here the Oblation is lifted over the Chalice and half of the Bread is dipped into the Chalice.

Let thy merciful kindness, O Lord, be upon us: like as we do put our trust in thee.[3]

---

[1] In the text follow the unintelligible words *quorum ut dixit*. For an explanation see Warren, *L.R.C.C.*, p. 262, note 89.

[2] These last three names are the second, third, and fourth Archbishops of Canterbury, which shows that there was intercourse between the Anglo-Saxon Church and the Irish. Note the absence of S. Augustine's name, due probably to hostility towards his policy in dealing with the Celtic bishops. This long list occupies folios 31*a*, 31*b*, and 32*a* of the original manuscript. [3] Ps. 33[21].

Here the Bread is broken.

They knew the Lord. Alleluia in the breaking of bread. Alleluia.[1]

The Bread which we break is the Body of our Lord Jesus Christ. Alleluia.[2]

The Cup which we bless (Alleluia) is the Blood of our Lord Jesus Christ (Alleluia) for the remission of our sins (Alleluia).[2]

Let thy merciful kindness, O Lord, be upon us. Alleluia, like as we do put our trust in thee. Alleluia.[3]

They knew the Lord.[4]

We believe, O Lord, we believe that in this breaking of the Body and by the shedding of the Blood, we have been redeemed, and we trust by partaking of this Sacrament we have been strengthened, that what we have through hope for the time being here [on earth] we may enjoy in the true fruits when we shall abide in heaven,[5] through our Lord.

Instructed[6] by the divine teaching, and following thy divine instruction we are bold to say:

Our Father, &c. . . .

    Deliver us from evil.

Deliver us, O Lord, from all evils past, present, and to come, and by the intercessions of thy blessed Apostles Peter and Paul, Patrick, mercifully grant peace in our days, that aided by the help of thy loving-kindness we may be ever set free from sin and secure from all disquiet; Through our Lord.

The Peace and love of our Lord Jesus Christ, and the Communion of all the Saints be with us always.

And with thy spirit.

Thou commandedst peace, thou gavest peace, thou didst leave peace: give us, O Lord, thy peace from heaven, and make this

---

[1] Adapted from Luke 24[35].   [2] Adapted from 1 Cor. 10[16].
[3] Ps. 33[21].   [4] Adapted from Luke 24[35].
[5] ut quod spe interim hic tenemus mansuri in celestibus veris fructibus perfruamur.
[6] Note difference between this and the Roman formula.

day peaceful, and the remaining days of our life do thou dispose in thy peace. Through our Lord.

May the Commixture of the Body and Blood of our Lord Jesus Christ be to us Salvation unto everlasting life. Amen.

Behold the Lamb of God
Behold, that takest away . . .
My Peace I give unto you.[1] Alleluia.
My Peace I leave with you.[1] Alleluia.
Great is the peace that they have who love thy law,
Alleluia; And they are not offended at it.[2] Alleluia.
Ruler of heaven with peace. Alleluia.
Full of the odour of life. Alleluia.
Sing ye a new song.[3] Alleluia.
All the saints come. Alleluia.
Come, eat of my bread, Alleluia, and drink of the wine which
    I have mingled.[4] Alleluia.
The Lord is my shepherd.[5]

Whoso eateth my flesh, and drinketh my blood, Alleluia, dwelleth in me, and I in him.[6] Alleluia.

The earth is the Lord's.[7]

This is that bread which came down from heaven.[8] Alleluia.
He that eateth of this bread shall live for ever. Alleluia.
Unto thee, O Lord, will I lift up my soul.[9]

He rained down manna also upon them for to eat: and gave them food from heaven, Alleluia. So man did eat Angels' food. Alleluia.[10]

Give sentence with me, O Lord.[11]

Eat, O friends: Alleluia, drink, yea drink abundantly, O beloved.[12]

Receive this sacred Body of the Lord, and the Blood of salvation, Alleluia, unto yourselves to eternal life. Alleluia.

My lips shall speak of thy praise: when thou hast taught me thy statutes.[13]

---

[1] John 14[27].   [2] Ps. 119[165].   [3] Or it may be Ps. 95[1].
[4] Prov. 9[5].   [5] Ps. 23[1].   [6] John 6[56].   [7] Ps. 24[1].
[8] John 6[58].   [9] Ps. 25[1].   [10] Ps. 78[24–5].   [11] Ps. 7[8].
[12] Song of Sol. 5[1].   [13] Ps. 119[171].

I will alway give thanks unto the Lord: Alleluia. His praise shall ever be in my mouth. Alleluia.[1]

O taste and see, Alleluia, how gracious the Lord is. Alleluia.[2]

Where I am, Alleluia, there shall also my servant be. Alleluia.[3]

Suffer little children, and forbid them not, Alleluia, to come unto me. Alleluia, for of such is the kingdom of heaven. Alleluia.[4]

Repent ye, Alleluia, for the kingdom of heaven is at hand. Alleluia.[5]

The kingdom of heaven suffereth violence, Alleluia, and the violent take it by force. Alleluia.[6]

Come, ye blessed of my Father, inherit the kingdom, Alleluia, prepared for you from the foundation of the world.[7]

Glory be. Come ye. As it was. Come ye.

The devotee of Caich wrote:[8]

Grant, we beseech thee, O Lord, that we who have been fed with this heavenly gift, may be cleansed from our secret sins, and delivered from the snares of our enemies. Through, &c.

We give thanks unto thee, O Lord, Holy Father, Almighty eternal God, who hast fed us with the communion of the Body and Blood of Christ thy Son; and we humbly implore thy mercy, O Lord, that this thy sacrament may not be to us for judgement to condemnation, but for pardon through the intercession of the Saviour, May it be a cleansing of sins, a strengthening of the weak, a support against the perils of the world; May this Communion purge us from sin, and make us partakers of the heavenly joys it gives. Through.

The Mass is finished.

In peace.[9]

[1] Ps. 34[1].   [2] Ps. 34[8].   [3] John 12[26].
[4] Matt. 19[14].   [5] Matt. 3[2].   [6] Matt. 11[12].
[7] Matt. 25[34].   [8] See Warren, *L.R.C.C.*, p. 267, note 184.
[9] 'The absence of any reference to the ablutions and the "last Gospel" is common in Missals before the twelfth century, the earliest evidence is given in the Early Eng. Text Soc. Vol. 71, pp. 301, 383.' Warren, *L.R.C.C.*

VI. THE BOOK OF DEER

Also a prayer before the Lord's Prayer.

O God, the Creator of all nature, and Author of all beginning both in heaven and on earth; receive the devout prayers of thy trembling people from thy throne of unapproachable light, and hear the prayers of undoubting expectation, among the surrounding Cherubim and Seraphim's unwearied praises.

Our Father . . . to the end.

Deliver us, O Lord, from evil, O Lord Jesu Christ, guard us ever in all good works, O fount and author of all good things, O God, empty us from faults, and replenish us with good virtues. Through thee, O Christ Jesu.

Here give the Sacrifice to him.

May the Body with the Blood of our Lord Jesus Christ be health and salvation to thee unto life everlasting.

Refreshed by the Body and Blood of Christ, let us ever say unto thee, O Lord, Alleluia. Alleluia. Alleluia.

For he satisfieth the empty soul: and filleth the hungry soul with goodness. Alleluia. Alleluia.[1]

That they would offer unto him the sacrifice of thanksgiving: and tell out his works with gladness. Alleluia. Alleluia.[2]

I will receive the cup of salvation: and call upon the name of the Lord. Alleluia. Alleluia.[3]

Refreshed by the Body of Christ. Alleluia. Alleluia.

O Praise the Lord, all ye heathen. Alleluia. Alleluia.[4]

Glory be to the Father.

Refreshed, &c. Alleluia. Alleluia.

Now and ever shall be.

Refreshed.

[1] Ps. 107⁹.   [2] Ps. 107²².   [3] Ps. 116¹².   [4] Ps. 117¹.

Offer the sacrifice of righteousness: and put your trust in the Lord.[1]

We give thanks unto thee, O God, through whom we have celebrated the holy Mysteries, and we earnestly desire the gift of holiness: have mercy upon us, O Lord, Saviour of the world. Who reignest world without end. Amen.

[1] Ps. 4[5].

VII. EXTRACT FROM THE BOOK OF DIMMA

Brethren, let us pray our Lord God for our brother N. whom the evil of grievous sickness at this time distresses; that the goodness of the Lord may vouchsafe to heal him with heavenly medicines. May he who hath given the soul, give also preservation. Through our Lord.

Dearly beloved brethren, let us humbly pray for our sick brother, to the Almighty living God, to whom it is easy to restore and establish all his good works; that either in refreshment or renewal the creature may feel the hand of the creator; in the man of his making may the living Father vouchsafe to re-create his work. Through our Lord.

O Lord, Holy Father, author of the universe, Almighty everlasting God, to whom all things live, who quickenest the dead and callest those who are not, as those which are, thou who art the artificer, affectionately perform thine accustomed work in this thy handiwork. Through our Lord.

Dearly beloved brethren, we beseech God in whose hand is the support of the living as much as the life of the dead; that he may heal the infirmity of this body and give salvation to the soul, that what by merit he does not deserve, he may obtain through our prayers for mercy's sake. Through our Lord.

O God, who willest not the death of a sinner but rather that he may turn and live, dismiss the sins of this man who with all his heart hath turned to thee, and bestow on him the grace of everlasting life. Through our Lord.

O God, who ever rulest over thy creation in righteousness; incline thine ear to our supplications unto thee, favourably behold thy servant N. toiling in adversity of bodily health, visit him in thy salvation of heavenly grace for medicine. Through our Lord.

The Lection of the Apostle to the Corinthians.

If in this life only . . . shall all be made alive.[1]

[1] I Cor. 15[19-22].

The same day . . . astonished at his doctrine.[1]

Instructed by the divine teaching and following divine instruction, we are bold to say:

I believe in God the Father Almighty.
And I believe in Jesus Christ his Son.
And I believe in the Holy Ghost.
I believe in the life after death.
I believe in my resurrection.

I anoint thee with the sanctified oil in the name of the Trinity, that thou mayest be saved world without end.

Grant unto us thy servants that praying with boldness, we may deserve to say: Our Father.

If the sick man can sing, he does, if not, the Priest sings for him.

Acknowledge, O Lord, the words which thou hast commanded, pardon the presumption which thou hast ordered; it is ignorance in us not to acknowledge our desert, [but] stubbornness not to keep the commandment whereby we are instructed to say: Our Father.

Here the Pax is given to him, and he says:

Deliver us, O Lord, from every evil, and guard us ever in every good [work]. O Christ Jesu, author of all good things, who reignest for ever.

The Peace and Communion of thy Saints, O Christ Jesu, be ever with us.

He [the sick man] responds: Amen.

[The Priest] gives him the Eucharist, saying:

The Body and Blood of our Lord Jesus Christ Son of the living God preserve thy soul to eternal life.[2]

After receiving, [the sick man] says:

We give thanks to God Almighty that us of earthly origin and nature by the gift of his Sacrament he hath quickened into heavenly motion.

[1] Matt. 22[23-33].
[2] Evidence for Communion in both kinds together.

Another prayer.

Shew us thy mercy, O Lord.[1]

Turn us, O God of our salvation: and vouchsafe to confirm our salvation. Who reignest world without end.[2]

Alleluia. I will receive the cup of salvation: and call upon the name of the Lord.[3]

Alleluia. The Lord is my strength, and my song: and is become my salvation.[4]

Alleluia. Refreshed by the Body and Blood of Christ, let us ever say unto thee.[5]

Alleluia. Praise the Lord, all ye heathen . . . *to the end.*[6]

Alleluia. Offer the sacrifice, of righteousness: and put your trust in the Lord.[7]

Then [*the Priest*] *signs* [*him*] *and says:*

Peace be with thee. The Lord bless thee, and guard thee, lift up his countenance upon thee, that he may give thee peace.

[*The sick man*] *responds:*

O God, we give thanks unto thee through whom we celebrate the holy Mysteries, and we earnestly desire from thee the gift of holiness, who reignest for ever.

[1] Ps. 85[7].   [2] Adapted from Ps. 85[4].
[3] Ps. 116[12].   [4] Ps. 118[14].   [5] See *Book of Deer*.
[6] Ps. 117.   [7] Ps. 4[5].

VIII. THE BOOK OF MULLING

A general prayer for the infirm begins.

Dearly beloved brethren, let us pray for the spirit of our beloved N. who after the flesh suffers sickness, that the Lord may shew him the revelation of sorrows, may grant him life, may bestow a safeguard of salvation, for a reward of good works. Through our Lord.

A general Preface begins.[1]

Dearly beloved brethren, let us pray for our brother N. who is vexed with trouble of the flesh and with sickness, that the Lord of his goodness would vouchsafe to visit and strengthen him with the medicine of heaven through the angel. Through our Lord ... Father Almighty, and spare this thy servant N. whom thou hast sanctified and redeemed with the great price of thy holy Blood, world without end.

A blessing over the water.

Let us pray and beseech mercy from the Lord, that he would vouchsafe to bless and to sanctify this font with the heavenly Spirit. Through our Lord.

Blessing of the man.

The Lord bless thee, and keep thee. The Lord make his face to shine upon thee, and be gracious unto thee, the Lord lift up his countenance upon thee, and give thee peace and health: have mercy, O our God. Amen.

Then he anoints him with oil.

I anoint thee with the oil of holiness in the name of God the Father, and of the Son, and of the Holy Ghost, so that thou shalt be saved in the name of the Holy Trinity.

Immediately he sings:

I believe in God the Father.

[1] See Warren, *L.R.C.C.*, p. 171, note 9.

Then is said to him that he may renounce all things:

O God the creator of all nature, and author of all beginnings in heaven and in earth, receive these devout prayers of thy trembling people from thy throne of unapproachable light, and hear the prayers of undoubting expectation among the surrounding Cherubim and Seraphim's unwearied praises.

Our Father.

The Collect now follows:

Deliver us from evil, O Lord Jesu Christ, guard us in every good work, author of all good things abiding and reigning world without end. Amen.

Then he is refreshed with the Body and Blood.

May the Body with the Blood of our Lord Jesu Christ be unto thee health to life eternal.

Prayer after receiving the Eucharist.

Guard within us, O Lord, thy glorious gift, that we may be for ever defended against all things of the present age, by the stain of the Eucharist which we receive our bodily strength may be built up. Through our Lord.

Alleluia.

That they would offer unto him the sacrifice of thanksgiving: and tell out his works with gladness. Alleluia.[1]

I will receive the cup of salvation: and call upon the name of the Lord.[2]

Refreshed by the Body and Blood of Christ, let us ever say to thee, O Lord, Alleluia. Alleluia.

O praise the Lord, all ye heathen.[3]

Glory be to the Father.

[1] Ps. 107[22].   [2] Ps. 116[12].   [3] Ps. 117[1].

Offer the sacrifice of righteousness: and put your trust in the Lord.[1]

We give thanks unto thee, O God, through whom we have celebrated the holy Mysteries, and we earnestly desire the gift of holiness; through our Lord Jesus Christ thy Son, to whom be glory world without end.

[1] Ps. 4⁵.

While the Priest puts on his Sacred Vestments to say Mass, he says the following hymn:

Come, Holy Ghost, our souls inspire,
And lighten with celestial fire; &c.

℣. Send forth thy spirit and they shall be made;
℟. And thou shalt renew the face of the earth.

Let us pray.

Almighty God, unto whom all hearts be open, &c.

Then follows the Antiphon:

I will go unto the altar of God.

Give sentence with me, O God, &c.[1]

The whole Psalm is said with Glory be to the Father, &c. *Then follows the Antiphon:*

I will go unto the altar of God, even unto the God of my joy and gladness.

Lord, have mercy upon us.
Christ, have mercy upon us.
Lord, have mercy upon us.

Our Father . . . deliver us from evil. Amen.

Hail, Mary.

When these things are finished and the Office of the Mass has begun, and after the Office Glory be to the Father, *the Priest goes up to the step of the altar with his Ministers, and himself says the Confession with the Deacon assisting on the right, and the Subdeacon on the left, beginning in this way:*

℣. And lead us not into temptation;
℟. But deliver us from evil.
℣. O give thanks unto the Lord, for he is gracious;
℟. For his mercy endureth for ever.[2]

[1] Ps. 43.   [2] Ps. 118[1].

I confess to God, to blessed Mary, and all the Saints, and to you, that I have sinned exceedingly in thought, word, and deed; through my fault; I pray holy Mary, all the Saints of God and you to pray for me.

The Ministers respond:

May Almighty God have mercy upon you, forgive you all your sins, deliver you from all evil, preserve and confirm you in goodness, and bring you to everlasting life.

P. Amen.

Afterwards they say the Confession, *to which the Priest says* May Almighty God, &c. *as above; then the Priest says:*

The Almighty and merciful God grant unto you absolution and remission of all your sins, and amendment of life, the grace and consolation of the Holy Ghost.

The Ministers respond: Amen.

℣. Our help standeth in the Name of the Lord;
℟. Who hath made heaven and earth.[1]
℣. Blessed be the Name of the Lord;
℟. From this time forth and for ever.[2]

Let us pray.

When these prayers are finished, the Priest kisses the Deacon, and afterwards the Subdeacon, saying:

Receive the Kiss of Peace and love, that ye may be fit for the holy altar, to perform the divine Office. *Then the Priest goes up to the altar, and says in a low voice in the midst of the altar, and with bowed body and joined hands:*

Let us pray.

Take away from us, O Lord, all our iniquities; that we may be worthy to enter the Holy of Holies with pure minds. Amen.

Then the Priest kisses the altar and raises himself; standing in the middle he signs himself on his face, saying thus:

In the Name of the Father, and of the Son, and of the Holy Ghost. Amen.

[1] Ps. 124⁷.   [2] Ps. 113².

*Then the Deacon puts the incense into the thurible, saying first
to the Priest:*

Bless.

P. O Lord. By Him be thou blessed in whose honour thou
shalt be burned. In the Name, &c.

*The Priest censes the altar, and is afterwards himself censed by
the Deacon. He then kisses the Book of the Gospels which the Subdeacon brings to him. After this the Priest reads the Office, i.e. the
Introit. It is read thus: the Office, the Psalm, the Gloria, and the
Office once again.*

[e.g. Easter.

When I wake up I am present with thee.[1] Alleluia; thou hast
laid thine hand upon me. Alleluia; such knowledge is too wonderful for me. Alleluia. Alleluia.[2]
Ps. O Lord, thou hast searched me out and known me: thou
knowest my down sitting and mine uprising; thou understandest
my thoughts long before.[3]
Glory be to the Father, &c.]

Then is sung the ninefold Kyrie.[4]

When the Gloria *is said, it is always begun in the middle of the
altar, by the Priest.*

P. Glory be to God on high;
Choir. And in earth peace, &c.

*Immediately afterwards the Priest signs his face with the sign of
the cross, and turning to the people says:*

The Lord be with you;
℟. And with thy spirit.

---

[1] Ps. 139[18].
[2] Adapted from Ps. 139[4-5].   [3] Ps. 139[1].
[4] There is no explicit rubric here, but the Kyrie certainly followed.

H

Let us pray.

Then follow the Collects, *as many as are appointed for the Office of the Day, but never more than seven.*

[*e.g. Easter.*

O God, who through thine only-begotten One, hast overcome death and opened unto us the gate of everlasting life; as by thy special grace preventing us thou dost put into our minds good desires, so by thy help bring the same to good effect. Through, &c.]

The Subdeacon goes through the midst of the Choir to read the Epistle, *in the Ambo.*

[*e.g. Easter.*   i Cor. 5⁷⁻⁸.]

During the Epistle two boys go to the pulpit to be ready to sing the Gradual.

[*e.g. Easter.*

This is the day which the Lord hath made: we will rejoice and be glad in it.¹

℣. Blessed are those that are undefiled in the way: and walk in the law of the Lord. Alleluia.²

℣. Christ our passover is sacrificed for us.³]

On special Feasts there follows the Sequence. [*Examples of these will be found in Warren,* The Sarum Missal in English.]

The Deacon censes the midst of the altar, and taking the Gospel Book from the altar, seeks a blessing from the Priest thus:

Pray, Sir, a blessing.

P. The Lord be in thy heart and on thy lips that thou mayest proclaim the Holy Gospel of God. In the Name, &c.

When the Gradual, Alleluia, or Tract has been said privately by the Priest, the Subdeacon shall receive the Bread, Wine, and water with the Chalice and prepare them for the administration of the Eucharist. A blessing on the water having been asked of the Priest in this form:

Deacon. Bless.

Priest. The Lord. May this water be blessed by him from whose side flowed forth blood and water. In the Name, &c.:

¹ Ps. 118²⁴.   ² Ps. 119¹.   ³ i Cor. 5⁷.

the Deacon proceeds to the Rood Screen to read the Gospel.

[*e.g. Easter.*

S. Mark 16¹⁻⁷.]

When the Gospel is finished, the Deacon returns to the altar and brings the Text to the Priest to be kissed. Meanwhile the Priest, standing in the middle of the altar, begins the Creed.

P. I believe in One God.

Choir. The Father Almighty, &c.¹

When the Creed is ended the Priest turning toward the people says: The Lord be with you;

℟. And with thy spirit.

Let us pray.

Then he reads the Offertory.

[*e.g. Easter.*

The earth trembled and was still, when God arose to judgement. Alleluia.²]

The Deacon presents the Chalice with the Paten. The Priest receives them and slightly raising them says:

Receive, O Holy Trinity, this Oblation which I an unworthy sinner offer in thine honour, of blessed Mary, and all thy Saints, for my sins and offences, and for the salvation of the living and of all the faithful departed. In the Name, &c.

Having said this prayer he replaces the Chalice on the altar, and covers it with the Corporal, and places the Paten in front of the Chalice. Then he takes the thurible from the Deacon and censes the Sacrifice, saying:

Let my prayer be set forth in thy sight as the incense: and let the lifting up of my hands be as an evening sacrifice, &c.³

Afterwards he is censed by the Deacon. Then at the right-hand side of the altar he washes his hands, saying:

Cleanse me, O Lord, from all defilement of my heart and body, that being cleansed I may be able to perform the holy work of the Lord.

¹ The sermon (if any,) followed at this point, although there is no rubric fixing it.   ² Ps. 76⁸⁻⁹.   ³ Ps. 141², ³, ⁴.

H 2

Then standing in the middle he says with bowed head and joined hands:

In the spirit of humility and with a contrite heart, may we be accepted by thee, O Lord, and may our sacrifice be so made in thy sight, that it may be accepted of thee this day and may please thee, O Lord my God.

Making the sign of the cross over the Sacrifice and his face, he says:
In the Name, &c.

Then turning towards the people he says in a low voice:

Brethren and sisters, pray for me, that my sacrifice and equally yours may be accepted by the Lord our God.

The Clerks respond privately:

The grace of the Holy Ghost enlighten thy heart and thy lips; and may the Lord deign to accept this sacrifice of praise at thy hands for our sins and offences.

Turning to the altar he says the Secrets, *in number and order as the Collects before the Epistle.*

[*e.g. Easter.*   Let us pray.

Receive, we beseech thee, O Lord, the prayer of thy people, together with the offerings of the sacrifice, that being consecrated in these Paschal Mysteries, they may by thy aid, avail to our eternal healing. Through, &c.]

When he has finished the Secrets, he says in a loud voice:
World without end. Amen.
℣. The Lord be with you;
℟. And with thy spirit.
℣. Lift up your hearts;
℟. We lift them up unto the Lord.
℣. Let us give thanks unto our Lord God;
℟. It is meet and just.

It is very meet and just, right and for our salvation, that we should at all times and in all places give thanks unto thee, O holy Lord, Father, Almighty everlasting God.

[*Proper Preface for Easter.*

And thee indeed at all times, but most chiefly on this day we ought to praise more gloriously; for Christ our Passover is sacrificed for us. For he is the very Lamb which hath taken away the sins of the world, who by his death hath destroyed death, and by rising again hath restored life. And therefore with angels and archangels, &c.]

At the beginning of the Salutation the Deacon gives the Paten to the Subdeacon to hold, until the Paternoster is said. It is covered with a veil (Offertorium).

Then immediately with joined hands and eyes raised the priest begins the Canon. He inclines until the words Thy Son our Lord.

Thee, therefore most merciful Father, we most humbly pray and entreat, &c.

[*The Canon is the same as in the Roman rite until after the Embolismos. To save space we do not give it here, but the reader should see the Roman Canon.*[1]]

(*After the Paternoster and Embolismos, the Priest breaks the Particle and makes three crosses over the Chalice, saying:*)

The peace ✠ of the Lord be ✠ always with ✠ you;
℟. And with thy spirit.

Holding the three Particles over the Chalice he says:

O Lamb of God, that takest away the sins of the world. Have mercy upon us. (*Twice.*)

O Lamb of God, that takest away the sins of the world. Grant us thy peace.

Placing the small Particle into the Chalice, he says:

May this holy commixture of the Body and Blood of our Lord Jesus Christ, be to me and to all who receive it, health of mind and body, and a saving preparation for worthily attaining unto life eternal. Through the same Christ our Lord. Amen.

[1] See Introduction, p. 12.

Before the Pax is given the Priest shall say:

O Lord, Holy Father, Almighty everlasting God, grant me
worthily to receive this most holy Body and Blood of thy Son our
Lord Jesus Christ, that I may by it be found worthy to obtain
remission of all my sins, and to be filled with thy Holy Spirit,
and to hold thy peace. For thou art God, and there is none beside
thee, whose kingdom and glorious Dominion abideth for ever.
Amen.

*Here the Priest kisses the right-hand side of the Corporal, and
afterwards the Deacon, saying:*

Peace be unto thee and unto the Church of God;
℞. And with thy spirit.

*The Deacon receives the Pax from the Priest and gives it to the
Subdeacon. Then to the Rulers of the Choir, and then to the rest. . . .
Meanwhile the Priest says these prayers privately, holding the Host
in his two hands:*

O God the Father, fount and source of all goodness, who led
by thy loving-kindness didst will thine only-begotten Son to
descend into this lower world for us and to take flesh, which I
unworthy hold in my hands (*let him incline towards the Host*),
I adore thee, I glorify thee, I praise thee with the whole in-
tention of my mind and heart, and I beseech thee, not to
forsake us thy servants, but to forgive us our sins, that we may
be enabled to serve thee, the only living and true God; with
pure mind and chaste body; through the same Christ our Lord.
Amen.

O Lord Jesu Christ, Son of the living God, and by the will of
the Father and the co-operation of the Holy Ghost hast by thy
death given life to the world; deliver me, I beseech thee, by this
most holy Body and Blood from all my iniquities and from
every evil; make me ever obedient to thy commandments, and
suffer me not to be for ever separated from thee, O saviour of
the world; who with God the Father and the same Holy Ghost
livest and reignest God, world without end. Amen.

Let not the sacrament of thy Body and Blood, O Lord Jesu Christ, which I an unworthy one receive, be to me for judgement and condemnation; but of thy goodness may it avail for the salvation of my body and soul. Amen.

Inclining towards the Host he says:

Hail evermore, most holy Flesh of Christ, to me above all things the sum of delight. May the Body of our Lord Jesus Christ avail to me a sinner as the way of life. In the ✠ Name, &c.

He receives the Body, and then says:

Hail evermore, most heavenly drink, to me above all things the sum of delight. May the Body and Blood of our Lord Jesus Christ avail to me a sinner as an eternal healing unto the life eternal. Amen. In the ✠ Name, &c.

Having communicated himself he covers the Chalice, and inclining says devoutly:

I give thanks unto thee, O Lord, Holy Father, Almighty everlasting God; who hast refreshed me with the most Sacred Body and Blood of thy Son our Lord Jesu Christ; and I pray, that this Sacrament of our salvation which I an unworthy sinner have received, may not be to me to judgement nor condemnation for my merits, but for the profit of my body and soul unto life eternal. Amen.

The Priest goes to the right-hand side of the altar with the Chalice between his hands, and the Subdeacon pours over his fingers a little wine and water. After the first ablution this prayer is said:

Grant, O Lord, that what we have taken with our mouth, we may retain with a pure mind and that from a temporal gift it may become to us an eternal remedy.

He washes his fingers in the bowl of the Chalice with wine poured in by the Subdeacon, and after drinking it, this prayer follows:

May this Communion, O Lord, purge us from sin; and make us to be partakers of the heavenly remedy.

Returning to the centre he places the Chalice down on the Corporal with the bowl over the Paten, and inclining himself, says:

Let us adore the sign of the cross, by which we have received the Sacrament of salvation.

Then he washes his hands; and afterwards says with his Ministers the Communion.

[*e.g. Easter.*

Christ our Passover is sacrificed for us. Alleluia.

Therefore let us keep the feast, with the unleavened bread of sincerity and truth. Alleluia, Alleluia. Alleluia.[1]]

Then having signed his face with the sign of the cross, he turns to the people, and slightly elevating his arms, and with joined hands, says:

> The Lord be with you;
> ℞. And with thy spirit.

And turning to the altar he says:

> Let us pray.

Then he says the Post-Communions *in order and number as the* Collects *before the Epistle.*

[*e.g. Easter.*

Pour into us, O Lord, the spirit of thy love, that those whom thou hast fed with the Paschal Sacrament, may by thy goodness be made to be of one mind. Through, &c.]

The last Post-Communion having been said, and having made the sign of the cross on his forehead, the Priest turns toward the people and says:

> The Lord be with you.

Then the Deacon:

> Let us bless the Lord.

But at other times the words are:

> Go, the Mass is finished.

[1] 1 Cor. 5[7-8].

These things having been said, the Priest bows down before the centre of the altar and with hands joined, says:

May the performance of my service be pleasing unto thee, O Holy Trinity, that this sacrifice, which I unworthy have offered in the sight of thy Majesty, may be acceptable to thee, and through thy mercy may be a propitiation for me, and for those for whom I have offered it. Who livest and reignest God, world without end. Amen.

Which being finished he raises himself, signing his face, saying:

In the Name, &c.

And having made an inclination, he comes down from the altar, and with his Ministers goes back to the Sacristy, in the order in which they came out from it. And immediately after, Thanks be to God. *Nones is begun in Choir, when it is said after Mass.*

The Priest while he is returning from the altar says the Gospel:

In the beginning . . . grace and truth. (John 1¹⁻¹⁴.)

PRINTED IN
GREAT BRITAIN
AT THE
UNIVERSITY PRESS
OXFORD
BY
JOHN JOHNSON
PRINTER
TO THE
UNIVERSITY